John Adams vs. Thomas Paine

Journal of the American Revolution Books highlight the latest research on new or lesser-known topics of the revolutionary era. The *Journal of the American Revolution* is an online resource and annual volume that provides educational, peer-reviewed articles by professional historians and experts in American Revolution studies, and is edited and managed by Todd Andrlik and Don N. Hagist.

Other Titles in the Series

The Invasion of Virginia 1781
by Michael Cecere

The Burning of His Majesty's Schooner Gaspee:
An Attack on Crown Rule Before the American Revolution
by Steven Park

Grand Forage 1778: The Battleground Around New York City
by Todd W. Braisted

The Road to Concord: How Four Stolen Cannon Ignited the Revolutionary War
by J. L. Bell

A JOURNAL OF THE AMERICAN REVOLUTION BOOK

JOHN ADAMS
VS.
THOMAS PAINE

RIVAL PLANS FOR THE EARLY REPUBLIC

JETT B. CONNER

WESTHOLME
Yardley

For Rosie

Westholme Publishing, LLC
904 Edgewood Road
Yardley, Pennsylvania 19067
Visit our Web site at www.westholmepublishing.com

First Printing November 2017
ISBN: 978-1-59416-292-3
Also available as an eBook.

Printed in the United States of America.

CONTENTS

PREFACE

THOMAS PAINE WAS MORE THAN A FAMOUS REBEL. HIS EARLY writings on American politics made substantive contributions to American political thought as well, something often overlooked. I argue in this book, which covers the period from 1776 to just before the Constitutional Convention convened in 1787, that Paine consistently projected a continental vision, that he proposed a dual system of governance with a strong national government, and that these and other ideas of his influenced constitution building in America. John Adams reacted vigorously and negatively to Paine's celebrated pamphlet *Common Sense* and its proposals to replace British rule with a democratic republic. He vowed to answer Paine's work, so I also suggest that Paine served as a catalyst to force Adams to declare publicly his principles and proposals for governing America by publishing his own pamphlet, *Thoughts on Government*. And because the two pamphlets veer off in different directions in their prescriptions for republican government, I thought it would be worthwhile to compare the rival tracts. An abridged version of *Common Sense* and the full text of *Thoughts on Government* may be found in the appendixes for easy reference.

Both pamphlets written in early 1776 anticipated key postrevolutionary questions about government in their time: the relationship between the national government and the states, questions about greater equality and broader representation of the people, the role of government in the economy, what to do about overbearing majorities and civic unrest, and the role of constitutions and the rule of law in a republic. These continue to be pertinent questions today. Even though historians and scholars have paid tribute to Paine's superb rebel rousing in *Common Sense*, giving him credit for helping to bring about the Declaration of Independence that summer, many have ignored his constructive ideas for forming constitutions and governments. Adams, instead, gets most of that credit; but he, for one, paid careful attention to Paine's proposals. And increasingly, he didn't like them.

Initially praising the "common faith" of revolutionary sentiments expressed in *Common Sense*, Adams later in life reappraised the pamphlet as a "poor, ignorant, malicious, shortsighted, crapulous mass."[1] Moreover, he had this to say about Paine and his legacy: "There can be no severer Satyr on the age. For such a mongrel between Pigg and Puppy, begotten by a wild Boar on a bitch Wolf, never before in any Age of the World was suffered by the Poltroonery of mankind, to run through such a Career of Mischief. Call it then the Age of Paine."[2] (Paine would sling his own mud at Adams: "His head was as full of kings, queens and knaves, as a pack of cards.")[3] And while Adams over time came to reappraise Paine's role in the American Revolution, what bothered him from the very start were Paine's "democratical" proposals in *Common Sense*, and their populist appeal.

Indeed, Adams eventually ridiculed Paine along with other writers who exploited a "Weakness in Mankind" when building their fame. In a letter to Thomas Jefferson in 1814, Adams wrote, "Nothing seizes the Attention, of the stareing Animals, so surely, as Paradox, Riddle, Mystery, Invention, discovery, Mystery [again], Wonder, Temerity." Adams tossed "Tom. Paine" into a group including Plato, Rousseau, Voltaire, and Hume, among others named, who had "too successfully grounded upon [the weakness of mankind] their Pretensions to Fame."[4] But as Adams was jealous of all who achieved fame by employing a popular voice (including Jefferson), he was especially envious of Paine.

In 1776, however, Adams took Paine's proposals seriously and published his own pamphlet soon after *Common Sense* to refute Paine's democratic proposals and to argue instead that Americans needed to preserve essential principles and features of the English constitution as they began to form their own governments. Adams never feared independence; what scared him was what might happen next.

What always struck me about Adams's pamphlet is that he directed his proposals toward the new colonial/state governments that were beginning to emerge in spring 1776, saying little about the nation or what form of government it should take, even though *Thoughts on Government* is so often credited with planting the seeds for our republican system of governance. Clearly, he wasn't thinking much that spring about a national constitution. Federalism, popular sovereignty, principles of "more equal" representation, recommendations for holding a national constitutional convention, a strong national government—all these seemed to be missing in Adams's early prescriptions for government in his pamphlet. But all these things, and more, can be found, even if only as rudimentary hints, in Paine's *Common Sense*. Nevertheless, Adams gets a lot of attention for his constitutional proposals; Paine not so much.

The late historian of the American Revolutionary period Pauline Maier downplayed Paine's role in Revolutionary America in her book *American Scripture: Making the Declaration of Independence*, writing, "Paine's influence was more modest than he claimed and than his more enthusiastic admirers assume." Limiting his influence to "the language in which Independence was justified," she nevertheless quoted Paine's observation in his *Rights of Man*, written over a decade after the event, that American independence was more than just a "separation from England . . . because it was accompanied by a revolution in the principles and practice of governments."[5] That Maier failed to follow up and even briefly explore Paine's contributions to those principles and recommended practices was, I believe, a significant omission from her book. John Adams, instead, got much of her credit for founding the American republic. Her assessment of Paine's and Adams's respective contributions to the American Revolution is rather typical: the first brilliantly (but only) supplied the revolutionary passion, the other the substantive ideas for governance. It's an assessment that's challenged in this book.

Authors always have some source of inspiration for their ideas or stories. Mine is as follows. Years ago I was invited to the home of Alpheus Thomas Mason for afternoon tea and to discuss my ideas about Thomas Paine's political thought. Mason, a leading scholar of the American Constitution, had recently retired and had given a guest lecture at a seminar on the Constitution that I was attending one summer at Princeton University. We briefly discussed Paine after his presentation. I pointed out to him that although his classic text *Free Government in the Making* acknowledged Paine's role in helping Americans reach the decision to declare their independence, it mostly ignored Paine's constructive contributions to American political thought. I explained that I thought Mason had accepted without question John Adams's often repeated dictum that Paine was better at tearing down than building up, and that just because Paine was indeed a noteworthy firebrand for independence we nevertheless shouldn't ignore the rest of what he had to say in *Common Sense*. Hence Mason's invitation to continue our discussion.

In his book, Mason wrote that *Common Sense* "was a call to arms, not a political treatise."[6] I argued that while his assessment was certainly true, there was much more to the pamphlet than a war cry. I thought it put forth several important ideas for constructing a constitution. Giving far more weight to the political thought of John Adams, Alexander Hamilton, James Madison, and other American founders, Mason delighted me by quoting lengthy passages from memory from Adams's *Thoughts on Government*, the *Federalist Papers*, and other works to bolster his claims about those founders who he thought had made the most significant contributions to American constitutionalism. But then he admitted he hadn't paid much attention to Paine's constitutional ideas in *Common Sense* and simply said to me, "Perhaps you're on to something. Why don't you write a book about Thomas Paine?" So, some forty years later, and after my own retirement from higher education, here goes.

Thomas Paine wasn't around for the Constitutional Convention of 1787. Neither was John Adams. Both were away in Europe at the time, on separate business. But their debate over republican principles that they began with the publications of *Common Sense* and *Thoughts on Government* informed the creation of America's first constitutions, state and national. I'm sure the late Alpheus Thomas Mason wouldn't see any reason to change his opinion that Adams was "certainly among the best informed men in the country on political science."[7] Adams was indeed learned and his recommendations for governance more consistent than the ideologically ambidextrous Paine, whose political philosophy continues to serve to this day as a model for both left- and right-handed hitters in American politics.

I believe that had Mason and Maier paid more attention to the political thought of Thomas Paine, both would not have so easily dismissed his contributions to founding a new nation during the Revolutionary period. He forced Americans to think beyond rebellion, and that, he believed, was the true achievement of *Common Sense*: "It was to bring forward and establish the representative system of Government," he wrote late in life, "that was the leading principle with me in writing that work, and all my other works during the progress of the revolution."[8] Paine would be disappointed to learn that the chief legacy of his pamphlet would not be its recommendations for governance. But one thing is for sure: those recommendations, along with those proposed by Adams in *Thoughts on Government*, helped Americans determine, on the eve of declaring independence, what kind of government should replace British rule.

One

"The Great Question" of Independence

MAKING HIS WAY FROM HOME IN THE TOWN OF BRAINTREE, Massachusetts, to Philadelphia to attend the next session of the Continental Congress in February 1776, John Adams stopped off at a bookstore in New York City long enough to pick up two copies of a new pamphlet, published anonymously, that was suddenly creating a buzz. Keeping one copy for himself, he sent the other back home to his wife, Abigail. He would have time to read his copy while continuing on to Philadelphia. Abigail was impressed with what she read, as she soon revealed to her husband, "I am charmed with the general sentiments of 'Common Sense,' and wonder how an honest heart, one who wishes the welfare of his country and the happiness of posterity, can hesitate one moment at adopting them."[1]

At first, John Adams also was impressed with *Common Sense*. "The Arguments in favor of Independence I liked very well," he recalled years later in his autobiography.[2] Responding to his wife's query about what he thought of the pamphlet, Adams said he was flattered to learn some people thought he was the author, although he "could not have written any Thing in so manly and striking a style." But as he mulled over the anonymous author's work, he started having second thoughts: "This Writer seems to have very inadequate Ideas of what is proper and necessary to be done, in order to form Constitutions for single Colonies, as well as a great Model of Union for the whole."[3] Whoever penned the piece, the author's proposals to eliminate the venerable and balanced English government of king, lords, and commons and replace it with a single house, popularly elected national legislature, rattled Adams. He was a rebel, too, but not this kind.

"Who is the author of *Common Sense*?" asked a writer in the *Philadelphia Evening Post*. "He deserves a statue of Gold."[4] It didn't matter, answered the unknown writer in a new and enlarged edition of the pamphlet published February 14: "Who the Author of this Production is, is wholly unnecessary to the Public, as the Object for Attention is the *Doctrine itself*, not the Man."[5] By March, the pamphlet was changing popular sentiments and the minds of some of the delegates in the Continental Congress as well:

> The pamphlet's usefulness was recognized by Congressmen, who sent copies to their home constituencies. [New Hampshire delegate Josiah Bartlett], for example, hoped that *Common Sense* would convince the people of Portsmouth, New Hampshire, who seemed terrified by 'the frightful word *Independence*.' . . . Rhode Island's Congressional delegate Samuel Ward went so far as to suggest that *Common Sense* should be 'distributed throughout all the Colonies . . . even at Public Expence. It has done immense Service.' He was told on good authority that two-thirds of the people of Pennsylvania, a colony which was officially dead set against Independence, 'are now full in his Sentiments; in the Jerseys & Maryland &c they gain ground daily.' . . . John Penn, a delegate who had recently returned to North Carolina reported (according to John Adams) that he 'heard nothing praised in the Course of his Journey, but Common sense and Independence. That this was the Cry, throughout Virginia.'[6]

Yet even as Adams and others soon discovered that the author was Thomas Paine, many were still left wondering about the man.

Oddly, Philadelphians had been reading him for almost a year in *Pennsylvania Magazine* and in several of the city's newspapers without knowing who he was because Paine had been writing anonymously for those publications, too, as was the custom in those times. Sometimes the writer used a pseudonym, though often there was no byline at all. But once Paine's name was revealed, about all that was known of him was that he had shown up in America just over a year before carrying letters of recommendation from Benjamin Franklin, whom Paine had befriended in England. A few knew also that he was editor of *Pennsylvania Magazine*, a publication that almost tripled its readership soon after Paine assumed control of its contents in early 1775. And now Paine's new pamphlet was sweeping the country, with thousands of copies already printed. Adams informed his wife that the pamphlet's writer was someone named "Payne."

On the same day *Common Sense* was advertised in the *Pennsylvania Evening Post*, January 9, 1776, the king's October 1775 speech to Parliament announcing an escalation of the war and warning of the deployment of "foreign" forces against the colonies also appeared in print for the first time, and in the same newspaper. What a happy coincidence for Paine and the publisher of his pamphlet, Robert Bell, who in a matter of days sold all one thousand copies of the first printing. But that was no coincidence, really, according to Paine. His bold call for independence from British rule and shocking attack against that "Royal Brute of Britain," King George III, not only hit any lingering hopes for reconciliation with the homeland squarely in the teeth, it was deliberately timed to coincide with the publication of the king's speech. "As I knew the time of the Parliament meeting, and had no doubt what sort of King's speech it would produce, my contrivance was to have the pamphlet come out just at the time the speech might arrive in America and so fortunate was I in this cast of policy that both of them made their appearance on the same day."[7] Paine not only had a gift for provocative writing, he demonstrated an instinct for marketing savvy as well.

In winter 1776, conditions were ripe for a new line of thinking in America. The undeclared war with Britain was rapidly approaching a year old, and the conflict showed no signs of abatement. Before war broke out the previous April at Lexington and Concord, the colonies had for a decade been engaged in a constitutional dispute with Parliament over taxation and representation and what they saw as other disturbing measures of colonial repression. Since the Stamp Act of 1765, Parliament had passed, then rescinded, then passed again new legislation designed to raise revenue from the colonies. Each piece of new legislation was viewed by the colonies as more burdensome than the previous measures. Rejecting these actions on grounds that Parliament was exceeding its constitutional authority by passing laws against the colonies without their consent, the colonies first challenged the authority of Parliament to pass such measures in the first place and then began, failing to gain any resolution with Parliament, to resist the measures directly. The famous Tea Party was such an example of resistance to the most recent tax measure Parliament had passed and the only one that had not been rescinded.

Britain began to fight back more aggressively against such resistance, though Parliament was divided over just how far Britain should push its case at the risk of going to war. Many in Parliament simply believed the government was exercising its legitimate sovereign authority over the colonies and that the Americans would eventually fall back in line and accept its measures. Instead, the colonies continued to debate and challenge that authority. Until spring 1775, America's beef with Britain had largely remained a constitutional conflict with Parliament. Then, as the dispute turned violent and the military conflict began to escalate, the colonies blamed the king's ministers for Britain's provocations. Many colonists assumed the Crown would step in and offer protection against Parliament's increasingly hostile actions. They were wrong.

Following the bloody battle at Bunker (or Breed's) Hill in June, which British troops won but with a heavy price paid in the loss of men and prestige, an alarmed King George III issued a proclamation in August declaring the colonies to be in a state of rebellion. Americans "have raised troops, and are collecting a naval force. They have seized the public revenue, and assumed to themselves legislative, executive, and judicial powers. . . . [T]he torrent of violence [against those who still retained their loyalty] has been strong enough to compel their acquiescence till a sufficient force shall appear to support them."[8] In addition to the promise of using "force," the proclamation justified further repressive measures against the colonies. Before the king's proclamation, the delegates of the Continental Congress had made an effort at reconciliation by passing its Olive Branch Petition, hoping that the conflict would subside and the monarch would intervene on their behalf. The petition concluded, "we most devoutly implore his divine goodness to protect us happily through this great conflict, to dispose our adversaries to reconciliation on reasonable terms, and thereby to relieve the empire from the calamities of civil war." (Just a week before, however, Congress had set in motion plans for an invasion of Canada.) King George refused to receive the petition.[9]

The phrase "civil war" is revealing. It demonstrates that Congress was not thinking about a war of independence, at least not yet. Those delegates such as John Adams who had attended the First Continental Congress and who continued to argue in the Second Continental Congress that reconciliation was futile remained in the minority, a status for them that stayed unchanged for almost another year. During that time, Americans continued to defend their rights as Englishmen and were not fighting for American independence.

In early July following Bunker Hill, George Washington, who had been appointed commander a few weeks before with the help of John Adams's nomination, arrived to take charge of the Continental Army. From Bunker Hill into early spring of the next year, Boston was a city under siege, General William Howe and his British troops having decided after Bunker Hill to shore up the city's defenses, hunker down, and await reinforcements. In the meantime, the Americans fortified their positions on the outskirts of the city and debated their options. As the standoff persisted, taking its toll especially on the British side with desertions, hunger, and disease, Washington agreed to a plan offered by a junior officer, Henry Knox, to get cannon that had been captured at Fort Ticonderoga and bring it overland to the American position. Washington was facing the end of enlistments of some of his army (something he always faced during the war), and he decided with the advice of his war council that a direct invasion of Boston was out of the question for the moment. Instead, he had been thinking about bombing Boston into oblivion.

It would take until March 1776 before the siege of Boston was over. Howe woke up early one morning and discovered great numbers of Knox's cannon trained down on the city, and him, from Dorchester Heights. In mid-March, Howe evacuated his troops from the city by ship. Abigail Adams wrote to her husband about watching the fleet leaving Boston, a scene she remarked that made the sea look like a forest.

In the meantime, the Continental Congress was back in session in February to continue the debate about what to do about the growing conflict. Delegates from the middle colonies—New York and especially John Dickinson of Pennsylvania—were still reluctant to consider independence. But outside Congress, thoughts of independence were now roiling the surface. The sudden appearance of *Common Sense* had blown off the lid holding down such ideas. Paine's pamphlet openly called on colonial America to break its bond with Britain immediately and create a republican government. And to the extent the pamphlet tipped America's glass toward independence, previously suppressed sentiments started pouring out in a flood, quickly reaching high levels. "Have You seen the pamphlet Common Sense? I never saw such a masterly irresistible performance. . . . [I]t will if I mistake not, in concurrence with the transcendent folly and wickedness of the Ministry give the coup de grace to G. Britain. . . . [I]n short I own myself convinced by the arguments of the necessity of separation," General Charles Lee wrote to General Washington.[10] For his part, Washington wrote to Lieutenant Colonel Joseph Reed that "the sound doctrine and unanswerable reasoning contained in the pamphlet *Common Sense* will not leave numbers at a loss to decide upon the propriety of separation."[11]

John Adams, though, wasn't so sure about the soundness of Paine's doctrines or his reasoning. What bothered him about *Common Sense* was not so much its call for independence. After all, he had been arguing in Congress since 1774 that reconciliation with Britain was a lost cause. In fact, Adams came to believe years later that what had been written in *Common Sense* was nothing new, was in fact something he had been saying all along in Congress: "The third part of *Common Sense* which relates wholly to the Question of Independence was clearly written and contained a tolerable Summary of the Arguments which I had been repeating again and again in Congress for nine months. But I am bold to say there is not a Fact nor a Reason stated in it which had not been frequently urged in Congress."[12] Upon reading the pamphlet for the first time, though, Adams immediately recognized that *Common Sense* had seized the moment by issuing a public call for action that would ignite the populace, and that worried him: "I dreaded the Effect so popular a pamphlet might have, among the People, and determined to do all in my Power, to counter Act the Effect of it."[13]

He was especially alarmed with Paine's recommendations for a radical form of republican government to replace British rule. His ideas were far too "democratical," said Adams. By early April, he started to circulate several letters at the request of several members of Congress, outlining what he thought governments in the colonies ought to look like. Clearly, Paine's pamphlet had been working on him. Adams referred to his own ideas as "sketches." Interestingly, Paine called his proposals for governance in *Common Sense* "hints." Both men were floating ideas yet to be fully developed. Adams wrote several versions of his letters, all with variations since he duplicated each of the ones that followed the original from memory. One letter, at the urging of Richard Henry Lee, was used as the basis for publishing a pamphlet, anonymously, in Philadelphia in April 1776, titled *Thoughts on Government, applicable to The Present State of the American Colonies*. It was Adams's effort to answer Paine's wildly popular pamphlet by countering Paine's plans for a democratic republic by publishing his own thoughts.

Common Sense had motivated Adams to compose a response, and when the response finally appeared in the spring, it was Paine's turn to be disturbed with what he read in *Thoughts on Government*. Recognizing immediately the completely different thrust of the pamphlet from his own proposals, Paine sought out Adams at his boardinghouse in Philadelphia to complain about the new pamphlet. Adams recalled the encounter in his autobiography:

> Paine, soon after the Appearance of my Pamphlet, hurried away to my Lodgings and spent an Evening with me. His Business was to reprehend me for publishing my Pamphlet. Said he was afraid it would do hurt, and that it was repugnant to the plan he had proposed in his Common Sense. I told him it was true it was repugnant and for that reason I had written it and I had consented to the publication of it: for I was as much afraid of his Work [as] he was of mine. His plan was so democratical, without any restraint or even an Attempt at any Equilibrium or Counterpoise, that it must produce confusion and every Evil Work. . . . This Conversation passed in good humour without any harshness on either Side, but I perceived in him a conceit of himself and a daring Impudence, which have been developed more and more to this day.[14]

Adams wasn't the only one responding to *Common Sense*. A flurry of pieces, some supportive of the pamphlet but most opposing it, appeared in the Philadelphia press in spring 1776. The most serious of these challenges appeared under the pen name Cato, who opposed independence and argued that reconciliation with Great Britain was compelled by constitutional premises. Writing under the name The Forester, Paine answered Cato in a series of letters in the Pennsylvania press that are known now as the *Forester Letters*. As this public debate over *Common Sense* continued in the spring, the discussion provided an additional backdrop for the movement toward independence taking place in Congress. Noticing that Cato addressed his essays "To the People of Pennsylvania," Paine, who had addressed *Common Sense* "To the Inhabitants of America," continued to explore the continentalist theme he had first announced in the pamphlet:

> The particular circumstance of a convention in Pennsylvania is undoubtedly Provincial, but the great business of the day is Continental. And he who dares to endeavor to withdraw this province from the glorious union by which all are supported, deserves the reprobation of all men. It is the true interest of the whole to go hand in hand; and dismal in every instance would be the fate of that Colony [which] should retreat from the protection of the rest.[15]

Since Pennsylvania was one of the last colonies still clinging to reconciliation in late spring 1776, Paine's message to its people was clear: only as a nation could America settle its account with Britain. Suggesting that "all men are republicans by nature and royalists only by fashion," Paine continued to sound the populist tone that would become the hallmark of his political thought, urging his readers to break the bonds with royal authority by changing their thinking. Reminding Cato, for example, that trial by juries is a republican institution since it is "a body of judges chosen among the people," Paine stressed that republican government meant the principle of popularly elected representatives.[16]

Adams remained conflicted about Paine's populist tone in the crucial spring of '76. *Common Sense* had come out of nowhere and overnight captured the public's attention, igniting a popular push toward independence while delegates in the Continental Congress were still debating the propriety of such an action. It was as though Paine had jumped on the bandwagon and taken the reins, just at the critical moment when the wagon was about ready to roll toward revolution, and then cracked the whip. Paine was just an opportunist, Adams later concluded, and had no background of his own for such a task. "[Paine] came from England, and got into such company as would converse with him, and ran about picking up what Information he could, concerning our Affairs, and finding the great Question was Independence, he gleaned from those he saw common place Arguments concerning Independence: such as the Necessity of Independence . . . the peculiar fitness at this time: the justice of it; the Provocation to it . . . our Ability to maintain it &c. &c."

Single-handedly, it seemed, Paine hijacked Congress's role by taking the arguments for independence directly to the public. That this development proved to be highly effective concerned Adams greatly. On the one hand, he admired the pamphlet's popular voice and revolutionary fervor. On the other hand, he fretted over the movement's accelerating pace and knew that the "Phenomenon in Philadelphia's" influence with the public was real.[17] Adams was going to have to find a way to help direct the movement's outcome, certainly by establishing the basic principles for the new American governments. His decision to publish his *Thoughts on Government* was designed to do just that.

Over time, these two revolutionaries, Adams and Paine, grew apart, with a rising—sometimes vitriolic—back-and-forth snipping between the two men that never eased.[18] With distance from the event later in his life, Adams denied Paine's influence on the Revolution and promoted his own. But both of their pamphlets, written in early 1776, started a critical debate on the eve of independence by offering rival plans that directly influenced the first governments of the new American republic, for both the new states and the nation. Adams realized he couldn't hold back the flood of revolutionary sentiments Paine had begun with his publication *Common Sense*, but he determined to find a way to shape its course, and with a new sense of urgency.

Two

Common Sense

BASED ON THE FIRST THIRTY-SEVEN YEARS OF HIS LIFE, NO ONE could have guessed that Thomas Paine would show up in Philadelphia in 1774 and in little more than a year publish a sensational pamphlet that would dramatically change America's future. Even Paine seemed surprised, as he later recalled:

> The world could not then have persuaded me that I should be either a soldier or an author. If I had any talents for either, they were buried in me, and might ever have continued so, had not the necessity of the times dragged and driven them into action. I had formed my plan of life, and conceiving myself happy, wished everybody else so. But when the country, into which I had just set my foot, was set on fire about my ears, it was time to stir. It was time for every man to stir.[1]

Common Sense quickly became the most widely read (or heard, by those who couldn't read) political tract written in America. Soon it was being translated into German for the German-speaking population of Pennsylvania as well as into other languages and distributed abroad. Of course, it found its way to England quickly. Paine estimated that one hundred twenty thousand copies of the pamphlet were printed in just a few months in America, though it's hard to know how he knew this since he gave up his copyright to the work and took no profits from sales, instead directing printers to pass along his earnings to help clothe Washington's wintertime soldiers in the Continental Army. The pamphlet was instantly successful and eventually became so well known that Paine, continuing to write anonymously, started using the title of the piece, or its initials, as a sobriquet in place of his usual pseudonyms. British soldiers, upon discovering a cache of Paine's papers after overrunning Fort Lee during their march into New Jersey in fall 1776, referred to Paine as that "scoundrel Common Sense."[2] In short order, Thomas Paine had become famous, or infamous, as the case might be, simply by writing powerful words that reached the people directly.

Sifting through the details of Paine's life in England before he arrived in America offers few promising clues for his future success. But "few" does not mean "none." Born in Thetford, England, on January 29, 1737, to a Quaker father and Anglican mother, Pain (he added the "e" to his surname, likely after arriving in America), grew up in a working-class family so poor it struggled to send him to grammar school, though with help from a relative the parents somehow managed to do so. (Paine had a sister who died in infancy.) There Paine spent six years learning grammar and practical skills but no Latin (his Quaker father was opposed), a component of a classic education for the college bound. At around age twelve, Paine's formal education ended and he joined his father's trade as an apprentice to become a corset maker, work he continued doing for seven years.

Soon after the beginning of England's Seven Years War with France in 1756, though, nineteen-year-old Paine, inspired by tales of the sea told by his former schoolmaster, left home and his apprenticeship to join the crew of a privateer ship. (Privateering was a form of licensed larceny on the high seas in times of conflict.) Just in time, his father managed to catch up with him in London to talk him out of it. That was a good thing because the English privateer the *Terrible*, commanded by a captain prophetically named William Death, soon engaged a French privateer at sea, the *Vengeance,* and the ensuing battle killed most of the crew on each ship, including both captains. But a few months later Paine tossed aside his father's cautions, as they "began to wear away" he later recounted, and embarked on yet another ship, the *King of Prussia*, a 340-ton privateer that sailed from London in January 1757.[3] This time, after completing a successful six-month cruise, young Paine disembarked with his own modest share of the ship's prizes, left his seafaring adventure, and struck out for London seeking new opportunities.

With his savings, Paine became a man of leisure, at least for a while, attending lectures on natural philosophy and hobnobbing with London's movers and shakers while making his rounds to the many coffeehouses and social clubs that had sprung up in the city. It was a brief interlude of self-education during years of an otherwise mundane, working-class existence. He later drew on the enlightened ideas acquired during this time when he eventually began a new career as a writer in America.[4]

His savings soon exhausted, Paine tried numerous careers (corset maker, teacher, Methodist preacher, tax collector, and tobacco, coffee, and grocery merchant) and two marriages, all of which eventually failed. But his lackluster accomplishments were marked with occasional signs of promise. For one, he developed and demonstrated a knack for debate and writing skills. And for another, he developed connections, one in particular that turned out to be very important for his—and America's—future.

After being reinstated to the Excise Service (he was previously fired from a former position with the service for certifying goods he had not personally inspected, a rather common practice among overworked and poorly paid excise men), Paine accepted the position of tax collector in Lewes, in 1768. This time he held the job for six years, one of the longest periods of his many careers. Several things stand out about these years. First, he dabbled in civic affairs. In addition, he developed a reputation as a very good debater, mostly after downing a few drinks at the White Hart Social Club, perhaps earning him another reputation that dogged him off and on for the rest of his life. But Paine was so gifted with verbal skills that more often than not he took home the trophy awarded by the Headstrong Club to the best debater of the evening.

Lewes was a hotbed of rumbling against the English social injustice issue of the day: the plight of the working class. Before long, Paine's fellow excise officers enlisted him, in 1772, to write a petition on their behalf pleading for higher pay. It was Paine's first political pamphlet, *The Case of the Officers of Excise*. He left his post in Lewes to have the pamphlet printed in London and circulated it himself among members of Parliament. The petition failed and cost Paine his job once again with the excise service, this time (formally) for having left his duties without leave, though it's more likely it was because of his efforts to organize the excise officers. But the pamphlet gave him his first real taste of political activism and demonstrated his passion and a talent for writing for a cause:

> Query, whether poverty has not too great an influence now? Were the employment a place of direct labor, and not of trust, then frugality in the salary would be sound policy: but when it is considered that the greatest single branch of the [tax] revenue, a duty amounting to near five millions sterling, is annually charged by a set of men, most of whom are wanting even the common necessaries of life, the thought must, to every friend to honesty, to every person concerned in the management of the public money, be strong and striking.[5]

In a noteworthy aside, a few years later in America, Paine wrote in *The American Crisis II* that he had never published a "syllable in England" prior to becoming a famous author in America. Technically, his claim was true since *The Case of the Officers of Excise*, though printed and circulated by Paine at the time, was not published and sold in England until many years later. But in his autobiography, John Adams seized on Paine's comment as evidence that his word could not be trusted.

The year 1774 was a turning point for Paine. He lost his last business to what was likely bankruptcy and lost his second marriage with it, resulting in a legal separation that remained in place for the rest of his life. Paine had met his second wife while working for her father. She was the daughter of a tobacco merchant. He married her soon after her father's death and continued to manage the business until it failed. "Trade I do not understand,"[6] he once remarked. But fortunately for him, upon the dissolution of the business and his marriage, the legal separation settlement with his wife provided him with some money. It was around this time that Paine, through his circle of friends, was introduced to Benjamin Franklin, who represented the interests of several American colonies in England and was then living in London. That proved to be the break he needed.

Paine must have impressed Franklin because he acquired several letters of introduction for "an ingenious worthy young man"—including one to Franklin's son-in-law Richard Bache—and soon booked passage on a ship to America. It was his chance to start life anew, at age thirty-seven. After a difficult voyage at sea during which most everyone on board acquired a fever (most likely typhus), Paine arrived in Philadelphia in November so weak he had to be carried off the ship. Because of the letters from his new friend, Dr. Franklin, Paine was immediately put under the care of a physician who got him off the ship and attended to his recovery. A lucky break indeed.

Once recovered, it didn't take long for Paine to engage in American affairs. As it happened, he frequented a print shop and bookstore owned by Robert Aitken, a recent immigrant from Scotland. The two struck up a friendship, and Aitken offered Paine the position of editor for a new publication he was launching, *Pennsylvania Magazine*. Before long, in early 1775, not only was Paine editing the magazine but he also was writing articles under various pseudonyms. (To this day, scholars are trying to sort out exactly what Paine wrote during those days of anonymous authorship.) Among other writers for the magazine was John Witherspoon, the president of the College of New Jersey, today's Princeton University. Reverend Witherspoon, like John Adams, eventually came to despise Paine and his ideas.

The famous shots that rang out in April 1775 at Lexington and Concord startled Paine like everyone else. Up to then, he had mostly avoided, by agreement with Aitken, polemical articles in the magazine. Most pieces covered such things as science and satire, poetry and practical topics, though a few did address controversial issues such as slavery, the justification for bearing arms, or preparations for a defensive war. Whether Paine wrote the latter articles is still debated, but one poem he certainly wrote, published in the July 1775 issue and titled "Liberty Tree," left little doubt about his feelings toward the rising conflict with Britain. The last few lines of the poem anticipate *Common Sense*:

> But hear, O ye swains ('tis a tale most profane),
> How all the tyrannical powers,
> Kings, Commons, and Lords, are uniting amain
> To cut down this guardian of ours.
> From the East to the West blow the trumpet to arms,
> Thro' the land let the sound of it flee:
> Let the far and the near all unite with a cheer,
> In defense of our Liberty Tree.[7]

Just who and when someone suggested to Paine that he write a pamphlet on the conflict with Britain remains uncertain. He later seemed to credit Benjamin Franklin, who urged him to write a history of the Revolution: "I had then [in October 1775] formed the outlines of 'Common Sense' finished nearly the first part; and as I supposed the doctor's design in getting out a history was to open the new year with a new system, I expected to surprise him with a production on that subject much earlier than he thought of; and without informing him of what I was doing, got it ready for the press as fast as I conveniently could, and sent him the first pamphlet that was printed off."[8]

But Dr. Benjamin Rush, a Philadelphia compatriot, also took credit for urging Paine to write the pamphlet. In later years, an elderly Rush claimed that most of the pamphlet, in fact, was written by him. That boast may a be sign of a cloudy, if not confused, memory, but certain things are clear. Both Rush and Paine later wrote that Rush feared authoring a pamphlet on the conflict because of potentially harming his medical practice. He had previously written an antislavery piece and was attacked for it in the press; because Paine may have written an antislavery article for the magazine also—something that is disputed by most scholars now, though he certainly held such sentiments—the two had struck up a friendship in Aitken's bookstore. Paine, at the very least, would have as editor accepted the antislavery article for publication in the magazine.

It's likely, though, that Rush was one of those individuals with whom Paine shared some early drafts of his new pamphlet. Rush did state he gave Paine the idea for the pamphlet's title, *Common Sense*. Paine initially planned to call his production *Plain Truth*. Ironically, *Plain Truth* was the title of one of several pamphlets answering and attacking *Common Sense* in spring 1776 from a Loyalist perspective. There is little doubt though that Rush was responsible for suggesting that Paine give his new pamphlet to the Philadelphia printer Robert Bell for publication, because Rush knew Bell would take the risk.[9] And so he did.

What is known for certain is that Paine sat down sometime in fall 1775 to work on *Common Sense*. The pamphlet was first advertised on January 9, 1776, and offered for sale at the publisher's bookstalls in Philadelphia on January 10. Paine agreed to pay the publication costs and to split the profits equally with Bell, having committed to passing along his share to support Washington's troops who were fighting that winter in Quebec. But soon after the pamphlet's appearance, he was dismayed to learn that Bell told two of Paine's associates who were sent to check into the publication's sales that there had been no profits, despite its price of two shillings, a price Paine thought was excessively high. Unhappy with this news, Paine sought out another publisher for a new and enlarged edition he was planning for *Common Sense*. He found William and Thomas Bradford in Philadelphia, who were willing to print the new version of the pamphlet, and on February 14, 1776, Paine's enlarged edition was published, this time with an offering of six thousand copies for a shilling each, exactly half of what Bell had charged for the smaller first edition. It was promoted as one-third larger than the original, at one-half the price, and became popular so quickly that the new publishers had to outsource some of the printing to meet demand.[10]

Soon after Paine changed publishers and continuing well into February, an advertising war between Bell and the Bradfords broke out in the Philadelphia newspapers, mostly in the *Pennsylvania Evening Post*, with both sides taking out sizeable advertisements to promote their edition of *Common Sense* and to deride the other's. Bell had decided to continue printing his original edition of the pamphlet as well as to publish a new, unauthorized, enlarged edition of his own, flaunting any sense of copyright, which was largely nonexistent in the colonies in any case. Not knowing what the Bradford enlarged edition would contain, however, Bell simply added previously published materials of Paine's, and some pieces not written by Paine, to the first edition of the pamphlet, and also advertised it as the new enlarged edition. The fact that this advertising war between the publishers continued for over a month speaks to the value all saw in the pamphlet and the money to be made. The advertising dispute also helped increase demand for the pamphlet. But the different printings and editions of the work, which proliferated rapidly with additional printers and into other cities, also led eventually to confusion about the publication history of *Common Sense* that has only been resolved in modern times.[11]

Originally, Paine had intended for *Common Sense* to be printed in newspapers as a series of letters. Perhaps realizing that newspapers might not print any or all of the pieces, or that it would lack continuity, he began to think of a pamphlet instead. (Benjamin Rush also took credit for suggesting to Paine that he publish the piece as a pamphlet and not as a series in the press.) The original edition, as published by Bell, contained four sections. The enlarged edition, as published by the Bradfords, what Paine called "A New Edition," added new material to the original body of the work, largely focusing on economic matters relating to American self-sufficiency; an appendix that explicitly addressed the aforementioned king's speech and offered more reasons for independence from Britain; and a piece specifically addressed to Quakers, urging them to drop their de facto support for Britain by continuing to hold onto their pacifist stance in the face of the rising threat of war.

Common Sense can be reduced to two essential messages: the necessity and reasons for breaking off the relationship with British rule

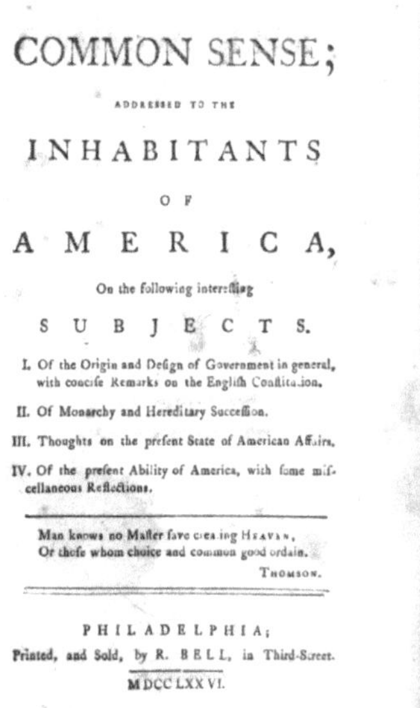

COMMON SENSE;

ADDRESSED TO THE

INHABITANTS

OF

AMERICA,

On the following interesting

SUBJECTS.

I. Of the Origin and Design of Government in general, with concise Remarks on the English Constitution.

II. Of Monarchy and Hereditary Succession.

III. Thoughts on the present State of American Affairs.

IV. Of the present Ability of America, with some miscellaneous Reflections.

Man knows no Master save creating Heaven,
Or those whom choice and common good ordain.
Thomson.

PHILADELPHIA;
Printed, and Sold, by R. BELL, in Third-Street.
MDCCLXXVI.

Thomas Paine (1737–1809) in a 1793 etching by William Sharp after a portrait by George Romney. (*New York Public Library*). Right, the title page of *Common Sense*. (*Library of Congress*)

and hints for what to do to replace it. Paine's first concern, his forceful and animated arguments for independence, made the pamphlet and its author famous. The second, his proposals for a republican government, got less attention (and still do), though Paine rightly foresaw that getting the colonists to begin thinking about that was a necessary step to achieving a separation from Britain. It was the second message, Paine's proposals for new governance, that also got Adams's attention.

The idea that *Common Sense* played a pivotal role in moving the nascent revolutionary movement toward independence is universally acknowledged today (though Adams lived long enough to eventually scoff at that thought). Franklin, Adams, and Alexander Hamilton—with varying degrees of conviction or caution—had also written favorably of separation, but their arguments failed to convince the public. Besides, these writings tended to focus on the colonies' deteriorating relationship with Parliament and not with the monarchy, the target for Paine's attack. For example, Adams, writing under the pen name Novanglus in several letters addressed to the people of Massachusetts in spring 1775, said:

> A union of the colonies might be projected, and an American legislature; for if America has 3,000,000 people, and the whole dominions 12,000,000, she ought to send a quarter part of all the members to the house of commons, and instead of holding parliaments always at Westminster, the haughty members for Great Britain must humble themselves, one session in four, to cross the Atlantic, and hold the parliament in America.[12]

This pervasive colonial obsession with the lack of representation of the colonies in Parliament—curious, as historians have pointed out there were large areas and cities in England, such as Manchester, with no representation at all either—summarized the stance taken by some leaders of colonial resistance as late as winter 1776. Some colonials, such as John Dickinson, felt that if the problem with Parliament could be resolved, then reconciliation was still possible, though Adams, Washington, and Hamilton, to name a few, had lost any such hope by that time. But until Paine published his pamphlet, America's struggle was over Parliament's oppressive—and what many colonies regarded as unconstitutional—regulations.

Common Sense simply and famously changed the subject. By placing the blame for America's woes directly and personally on King George III's shoulders, though he wasn't specifically named in the pamphlet, Paine personified the conflict. What really caught Americans off guard, and their attention at the same time, was the explosive way he attacked the British monarch and not just the monarchy. Describing the king as a "sullen Pharaoh," "wretch," "crowned ruffian," and just "a man," Paine sought to knock the monarch off his high throne.[13] American pamphlets of the eighteenth century were full of satire, but Paine's personal attack on the king was simply over the top for the times. Dismissing the legitimacy of the current line of British kings, Paine had this to say of William the Conqueror: "A French bastard landing with an armed banditti, and establishing himself king of England against the consent of the natives, is in plain terms a very paltry rascally original." And this: Nature disapproved of hereditary monarchy because "otherwise she would not so frequently turn it into ridicule, by giving mankind an *ass for a lion.*"

Paine's polemic against monarchy was, of course, not new, but the pitch and target of his attack were. The case had been made from the pulpits to the press in America, but no one had openly ridiculed George III by calling him names quite like Paine. The bombastic charges against the king certainly contributed to the pamphlet's surging popularity. But there was more.

Appealing to his Bible-reading, mostly Protestant audience, Paine equated monarchy with the "popery of government" and selectively quoted Old Testament scripture suggesting that the Bible condemned monarchy as "one of the sins of the Jews." (John Adams later assailed these arguments as "ridiculous" in his autobiography.)[14] Then turning to the natural order of things and aiming toward those holding a more enlightened view, Paine reasoned that "there is something absurd in supposing a continent to be perpetually governed by an island." It was contrary to the laws of nature: "In no instance hath nature made the satellite larger than its primary planet." As to the principle of hereditary succession, Paine simply appealed to empirical evidence: experience showed that "virtue is not hereditary."

What about the colonists' allegiance as British subjects to the current king? Paine offered an answer: "But admitting that we were all of English descent, what does it amount to? Nothing. Britain, being now an open enemy, extinguishes every other name and title: And to say that reconciliation is our duty, is truly farcical. The first king of England, of the present line (William the Conqueror) was a Frenchman, and half the peers of England are descendants from the same country; wherefore by the same method of reasoning, England ought to be governed by France."

And what about Britain's venerable constitutional principle of checks and balances? The English constitution, he argued, really represented:

> the base remains of two ancient tyrannies [monarchical and aristocratic], compounded with some new republican materials . . . in the persons of the commons, on whose virtue depends the freedom of England. . . . But as the same constitution which gives the commons a power to check the king by withholding the supplies, gives afterwards the king a power to check the commons, by empowering him to reject their other bills; it again supposes that the king is wiser than those whom it has already supposed to be wiser than him. A mere absurdity!

Paine's attack on "mixed government" and checks and balances was deeply troubling to John Adams; this fundamental difference in republican principles between the two revolutionaries easily led to the dispute that soon arose between them as they mulled over how to structure American governments.

Having thrown every argument he could think of against those with lingering hopes for reconciliation and colonial attachments to the Crown and homeland, Paine turned to his second concern, American governance. This was the crux of the problem, he considered, a "fear" he believed was holding up an outright declaration of independence. Americans hadn't thought much about what kind of government should replace British rule, he reasoned, so *Common Sense* offered some proposals, which Paine called "hints." Paine opened *Common Sense* with Lockean-like pastoral images about the origin of government. "Some convenient tree will afford [people] a State-House, under the branches of which the whole colony may assemble to deliberate on public matters. . . . In this first parliament every man, by natural right will have a seat." But as a colony grows, it becomes necessary to turn to a representative system, based on consent and periodic elections. "And as this frequent interchange will establish a common interest with every part of the community, [the people] will mutually and naturally support each other, and on this (not on the unmeaning name of king) depends the *strength of government, and the happiness of the governed*." As we'll see in the next chapter, "happiness" also appeared often in Adams's *Thoughts on Government*.

Government was a necessary evil because of the inability of moral virtue to rule society's affairs. The true end of government was freedom and security, and the least amount of government necessary to secure those ends was the best, a position that resonates with today's less-government-is-more crowd. Furthermore, *Common Sense* promoted simplicity: "I draw my idea of the form of government from a principle in nature . . . that the more simple any thing is, the less liable it is to be disordered, and the easier repaired when disordered."

In the third section of the pamphlet, titled "Thoughts on the Present State of American Affairs," Paine outlined his hints for American governance. He opened his discussion with this short but pregnant statement: "LET the assemblies be annual, with a President only. The representation more equal. Their business wholly domestic, and subject to the authority of a Continental Congress." Within these few lines, Paine revealed much of his thinking about republican government. The venerated English constitutional principle of mixed government in the form of king, lords, and commons disappeared. In its place was his suggestion for annually elected representative assemblies, without an independent executive. Furthermore, representation should be "more equal," i.e., more democratic. There was even a hint of federalism, by restricting provincial legislative authority to domestic matters and subordinating it to a national assembly whose business would be national and international in scope.

What immediately followed this opening of the subject was a sketch of governance for the colonies and for the nation and how these should originate. Paine outlined a system of representation for a large, national, single-body Congress, including a scheme for executive leadership of Congress dependent on the principle of rotation among the colonies. He recommended the use of an extraordinary majority, "not less than three fifths of the Congress to be called a majority," in order to pass legislation, a proposition interestingly presaging the longstanding cloture rule in the US Senate, essentially a rule requiring sixty votes and not a mere majority to get meaningful legislation passed in that body. And he called for a "continental conference," to frame a "Continental Charter, or Charter of the United Colonies." This continental gathering—or, in other words, a constitutional convention—would be an intermediary body between the government and the governed, comprising representatives selected by a combination of qualified voters and legislative assemblies or conventions held in each colony for the purpose. Paine suggested five delegates be elected by the public and four come from the representative assemblies. (Note the balance between those delegates elected at large versus those who were representatives in the assemblies.) This alone would make the representation "more equal." The gathering would create a charter that would establish the basis of representation for both Congress and the colonial assemblies, "drawing the line of business and jurisdiction between them: Always remembering, that our strength is continental, not provincial." It also would secure the rights of "freedom and property to all men, and above all things, the free exercise of religion"—something akin to a Bill of Rights.

Paine had not forgotten the king: "But where, says some is the King of America? I'll tell you, friend, he reigns above, and doth not make havoc of mankind like the royal brute of Great Britain." Let the charter, in a ceremony, rest on divine law, the word of God, said Paine, and "a crown be placed thereon, by which the world may know, that so far as we approve of monarchy, that in America THE LAW IS KING." And that law, Paine hinted in the passage, was a written constitution, a document that one could hold and place next to the family Bible. He concluded his thoughts on government by saying, "A government of our own is our natural right," and then he exhorted Americans to take a stand against Britain with these stirring words:

> O ye that love mankind! Ye that dare oppose, not only the tyranny, but the tyrant, stand forth! Every spot of the old word is over-run with oppression. Freedom hath been hunted round the globe. Asia, and Africa, have long expelled her.—Europe regards her like a stranger, and England hath given her warning to depart. O! receive the fugitive, and prepare in time an asylum for mankind.[15]

Constitutional scholar Edward S. Corwin said of Paine's scheme in *Common Sense,* "In this singular mixture of sense and fantasy, so characteristic of its author, are adumbrated a national constitutional convention, the dual plan of our federal system, a national bill of rights, and 'worship of the Constitution'; and this was some months before the earliest state constitution."[16] Commenting on Paine's style, historian Bernard Bailyn wrote, "The 'daring impudence,' the 'uncommon frenzy' which gave *Common Sense* its unique power, Paine brought with him from England in 1774; it had been nourished in another culture, and was recognized at the time to be an alien quality in American writing." And though the pamphlet displayed some of the "peculiar emotional intensity" of a Jonathan Swift, Bailyn remarked, it was also, as were all of the most effective American pamphlets of the era, designed to be expository as well as to persuade.[17]

Even as *Common Sense* was urging Americans to free themselves from British rule, Paine knew it was also necessary to explain to them what they had to do beyond the revolution to establish a free government on their own. Since the pamphlet directed the blame for America's problems away from Parliament and onto the monarch, Paine extolled the virtue of complete legislative supremacy. There would be no independent executive power; instead, executive authority resided completely within and was accountable to a legislature. However, the selection of those to exercise executive authority in the national Congress was left to the Congress, using this recommendation: "Each Congress to sit and to choose a president by the following method. When the delegates are met [in Congress], let a colony be taken from the whole thirteen colonies by lot, after which let the whole Congress choose (by ballot) a president from out of the delegates of *that* province." Then the process would be repeated, excluding those colonies that already had had a president serve, until all colonies had passed through their rotation. In summary, the executive was directly accountable to the Congress. Paine's scheme hinted of national executive authority insofar as there were any real powers there, and not colonial control of the executive authority in Congress, not even from that colony whose delegate had been chosen by Congress to serve as the executive leader for that year.

Both the Congress and the colonial assemblies should be single-body assemblies. Paine suggested a scheme of representation that gave the national Congress 390 delegates. He did not prescribe the powers of colonial legislatures, but he did restrict their authority to "wholly domestic" matters and he made that authority "subject to the authority of a Continental Congress," essentially giving the national congress a veto power. As to the powers of each (colonial assemblies and the Continental Congress), Paine suggested they would be derived from a "Continental Charter, or Charter of the United Colonies." And he left it to the charter to fix "the number and manner of choosing members of Congress, members of Assembly, with their date of sitting, and drawing the line of business and jurisdiction between them: Always remembering, that our strength is continental, not provincial."

It is clear from his words that from the beginning, Paine was among those—including George Washington, James Madison, Alexander Hamilton, and John Jay—who would soon come to be called nationalists, those, in other words, who held a continentalist vision and a national perspective.[18] And he was prescient about the way America should go about dividing national and colonial powers: Their respective powers were to be derived from a single, national charter (constitution), a hint that anticipated how the Constitution of 1787 would be structured to authorize and restrict national and state powers. The charter, in other words, both granted and limited powers within the context of a federal system of government, with the national governing body, the Congress, having superior powers over the colonial assemblies.

Paine said nothing in *Common Sense* about a judiciary, independent or otherwise. But he repeated his concern that a national charter ought to secure several rights, namely freedom, property, and "the free exercise of religion, according to the dictates of conscience." And he wrote that his proposal for a national charter would serve only as a temporary arrangement for American governance: After the continental meeting was over, it was necessary that the conference "dissolve, and the bodies which shall be chosen conformable to the said charter, [were] to be the legislators and governors of this continent for the time being." This last thought was in keeping with Paine's and Jefferson's belief, expressed later in their writings, that the form of government was a creature of the generation that created it, and it was up to future generations to keep or change it as they determined. Paine abhorred the principle that the living should be ruled by the dead, or that a constitution was somehow fixed in perpetuity without the possibility of change.

Paine always believed that the republican principles he laid out in *Common Sense* were more important than the pamphlet's arguments for independence, a thought seemingly at odds with the many historians and political scientists since his time who have focused only on the pamphlet's role in propelling Americans to declare independence. However, several scholars have acknowledged Paine's own appraisal of his pamphlet:

> The mere independence of America . . . were it to have been followed by a system of government modelled after the corrupt system of English Government, would not have interested me with the unabated ardor it did. It was to bring forward and establish the representative system of government, as the work itself will show, that was the leading principle with me in writing.[19]

And though *Common Sense* offered only "hints" as to what those republican principles ought to be, they were certainly instructive enough to horrify John Adams. The more he thought about Paine's proposals, the more Adams determined to counteract the potential effects that such simple and "democratical" ideas might have on the people. What Paine had done with *Common Sense* was to force Adams and others to think immediately about what kind of government should replace British rule. Paine, wrote historian Pauline Maier, "wanted to shift the focus of public debate from evaluations of British rulers and the prospects for reconciliation to deciding how an independent America should be governed. And that he did."[20]

It took Adams several months before he answered Paine in print by publishing his own pamphlet and offering a scheme quite different from that put forth in *Common Sense*. But Paine's plans ensured that

Adams would indeed follow through with his promise to counteract the effects of *Common Sense* by putting down some thoughts of his own. And a few months after Paine's pamphlet appeared, Adams answered Paine by publishing *Thoughts on Government*.

Three

Thoughts on Government

SOMETIME AFTER JOHN ADAMS AND THE MASSACHUSETTS delegation arrived in Philadelphia in February 1776 to attend the next session of the Continental Congress, he and the Congress learned that the previous December, Parliament had passed what has come to be known as the Prohibitory Act. The act banned all trade by the colonies with any foreign country and declared that any American ships found engaging in such trade would be seized. The legislation simply formalized what already had been going on in practice for some time. But Adams wrote to American general Horatio Gates that for all practical purposes, Britain had obliged the colonies by declaring independence for them:

> I know not whether you have seen the Act of Parliament call'd the restraining Act, or prohibitory Act, or piratical Act, or plundering Act, or Act of Independency, for by all these Titles it is called. I think the most apposite is the Act of Independency, for the King Lords and Commons have united in Sundering this Country and that I think forever. It throws thirteen Colonies out of the Royal

> Protection, levels all Distinctions and makes us independent in Spight of all our supplications and Entreaties. It may be fortunate that the Act of Independency should come from the British Parliament rather than the American Congress: But it is very odd that Americans should hesitate at accepting Such a Gift from them.[1]

Upon returning to the Congress, Adams knew that a number of the delegates were still not ready to separate from Great Britain. Many of the colonial governments had instructed their delegations that any vote for independence was prohibited. But Congress did soon retaliate against the Prohibitory Act by granting letters of marque to American ships, thus permitting them to act as privateers and seize the cargoes of British vessels. Furthermore, Congress took the additional step of closing American ports to British shipping and, on April 6, opening colonial ports to world trade. Those actions, of course, were the final nails in the coffin of reconciliation. And though Paine's *Common Sense* was working its magic on a few delegates who still were harboring thoughts of peace, Adams knew his work was cut out for him to persuade some members of Congress to change their thinking about "independency." He, like Paine, knew it was also necessary to get the delegates in Congress to start thinking beyond independence, toward the endgame—namely, what kind of government should replace Britain's. The opportunity came when several delegates approached Adams to gain his thoughts on how they should reorganize their colonial governments.

John Adams had been a member of the Congress since 1774 (the First and then the Second Continental Congress beginning in 1775). Unlike Paine, he had a considerable track record of accomplishments. Harvard educated and well versed in the classics, Adams was born in America. He had been a critic of British rule for some time. Growing up in an ordinary farmhouse in Braintree, Massachusetts, he had become an accomplished lawyer after some initial thoughts, and family pressure, to become a minister. By the time he entered the Continental Congress, he brought with him persuasive talents that would make him "one of the most 'sensible and forcible' figures in the whole patriot cause."[2] Notably, even though a patriot, Adams had in 1770 agreed to head the defense team for soldiers indicted for killing five citizens during the Boston Massacre. In spite of what might have been a risky move for his reputation to defend the soldiers, Adams was elected to the state legislature a few months after agreeing to defend them. It was the start of almost a decade of legislative service, first at home and then in the Continental Congress. The soldiers were acquitted.

It was Adams, after Lexington and Concord in April 1775, who persuaded Congress to appoint George Washington to lead the Continental Army. Like Paine, Adams was a revolutionary, but by comparison a more guarded one:

> While completely committed to secession from the British Empire, he thought there had to be a conspicuous consensus within the American citizenry for the revolution to succeed. And popular opinion needed to 'ripen on the vine' before that consensus became convincingly clear. Moreover, the transition from British colonies to American states must occur seamlessly rather than traumatically. . . . He wanted to orchestrate, if you will, an evolutionary revolution, to control the explosion.[3]

Early in spring 1776, several delegates in the Congress from North Carolina, New Jersey, and Virginia asked Adams for his ideas on establishing the proper form of government for their respective colonies. Initially writing out his thoughts for the North Carolina delegates, Adams then made copies of the original over several weeks, from memory, and provided one each to the delegates requesting them. Richard Henry Lee of Virginia asked Adams if he could publish his copy of the letter as a pamphlet and Adams agreed, provided it was done anonymously. Lee's copy was used to produce *Thoughts on Government*, published in April in Philadelphia.[4]

Adams first proposed that the end of government was "the happiness of society."[5] In fact, he used the word "happiness" often in the pamphlet. It was the happiness of society, which he refined to mean happiness for the greatest number of its members—anticipating the utilitarianism of Jeremy Bentham—for which government was founded, based on the principle "that the form of government, which communicates ease, comfort, security, or in one word happiness to the greatest number of persons, and in the greatest degree, is the best." And since the happiness of man rested on virtue, according to all moral philosophies, "Pagan and Christian," then that government which rested on a foundation of virtue would be better in achieving human happiness than any other form.

Governments could also be founded on the basis of fear or honor, but Adams argued that Americans would reject a government founded on fear as too brutal and "stupid." And while honor was a virtue, it was a lesser moral excellence than virtue (echoing a hierarchy of moral values taught by the classical political philosophers), so only that form of government that reflected the noblest virtues of humankind would likely produce human happiness, and that form was a republic. Furthermore, the best republic was one based on laws:

> [T]here is no good government but what is Republican. . . . [T]he only valuable part of the British constitution is so; because the very definition of a Republic, is "an Empire of Laws, and not of men." . . . [A]s a Republic is the best of governments, so that particular arrangement of the powers of society, or in other words that form of government, which is best contrived to secure an impartial and exact execution of the laws, is the best of Republics.[6]

There were many kinds of republics, Adams wrote. In a large society "inhabiting an extensive country" where it was not possible for the multitude of people to gather to make laws, such as America, it was necessary to "depute power from the many, to a few of the most wise and good." This kind of republic required a system to choose representatives. The colonies had to either set the number and qualifications of those who would choose the representatives or "annex this priviledge to the inhabitants of a certain extent of ground." Once decided, the "principal difficulty lies, and the greatest care should be employed in constituting this Representative Assembly." Adams argued that the assembly must be, "in miniature, an exact portrait of the people at large," a theme he returned to later when discussing

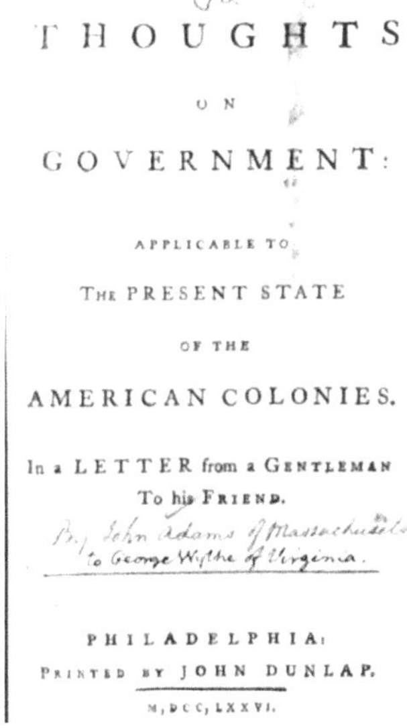

THOUGHTS

ON

GOVERNMENT:

APPLICABLE TO

THE PRESENT STATE

OF THE

AMERICAN COLONIES.

In a LETTER from a GENTLEMAN

To his FRIEND.

PHILADELPHIA:

PRINTED BY JOHN DUNLAP.

M,DCC,LXXVI.

John Adams (1735–1826) in the 1793 official presidential portrait by John Trumbull. (*The White House*) Title page of *Thoughts on Goverment.* (*Library of Congress*)

equality. But an important question arose when thinking about a single assembly, "whether all the powers of government, legislative, executive, and judicial, shall be left in this body?"

Undoubtedly thinking of Paine's recommendations in *Common Sense* for a single-chamber legislative body, Adams rejected the model for the colonies. He offered several reasons for his objections to a unicameral legislature. Among these, a single assembly would be "liable to all the vices, follies and frailties of an individual"; such an assembly would be "avaricious" and likely would burden, "without compunction," its constituents; and a "single Assembly, possessed of all the powers of government, [would] execute all laws arbitrarily for their own interest." Instead of Paine's "simple" form of government, one with a single legislative assembly, Adams recommended a model where the legislative power was "complex." In fact, he sketched a "tricameral" legislative model (three branches). But if the devil is in the details, only two of these legislative bodies are clearly described: a representative assembly and smaller "distinct Assembly," which is "vested with the executive power." This "Council" should be elected by the larger assembly, but then should have "a free and independent exercise of its judgment, and consequently a negative voice in the legislature."

Returning to his thoughts on balanced government, Adams suggested the creation of an executive power, a governor, who should be chosen by the legislatures and subject to annual election, and who should "be made also an integral part of the legislature." Though such an executive would not be entirely independent (being part of the legislature), the governor should have "a negative upon the legislative." Among the governor's powers should be the command of colonial militias and the power of pardons. In effect, these recommendations provided for an executive veto over legislation, made the chief executive the commander in chief, and located the power to pardon in executive authority. These "negatives" were Adams's way of making checks and balances work.

Turning to the judicial power, something Paine had ignored in *Common Sense*, Adams recommended that judicial officers, along with "other officers, civil and military," be "nominated and appointed by the Governor, with the advice and consent of Council." The judicial power "ought to be distinct from both the legislative and executive, and independent upon both, so that it may be a check upon both, as both should be checks upon that." The scheme Adams proposed was not only a feature of his "complex" government structure but was designed to further balance powers. Judges should hold their offices for life, "during good behavior." They would be subject to impeachment: The "House of Representatives, should impeach them before the Governor and Council, where they should have time and opportunity to make their defence." If convicted, they could be removed from office and face additional punishment "as shall be thought proper."

In addition to these proposals, Adams offered thoughts on other areas of government and its responsibilities, many not addressed directly by Paine in his pamphlet. He spoke of sheriffs and how they should be chosen "by the freeholders of counties," as should county clerks and other such officers. He urged the colonies to pass militia laws, "requiring all men, or with very few exceptions, besides cases of conscience, to be provided with arms and ammunition" and be provided training. He proposed that the colonies provide educational opportunities for youth, especially the youth of the "lower class of people." He raised the idea of passing sumptuary laws, laws that would regulate luxurious living, though he knew this idea would "excite a smile." Such laws might be used for the purpose of achieving sufficient revenue savings to support the ongoing war with Britain: "Frugality is a great revenue, besides curing us of vanities, levities and fopperies which are real antidotes to all great, manly and warlike virtues." Exactly how these laws might function he did not address in his pamphlet, but a tax on the rich might be what he had in mind.

Finally, he proposed that all commissions, writs, indictments, and other legal proceedings be done in the name of the colonies instead of the king. Adams, after all, was a lawyer and committed rebel. All of these suggestions, up to this point in his pamphlet, were aimed specifically at the colonies and their powers. That, of course, is what the delegates who asked for his thoughts were seeking. Then Adams devoted only two sentences in *Thoughts on Government* to creating a national government. He offered this advice:

> If the Colonies should assume governments separately, they should be left entirely to their own choice of the forms, and if a Continental Constitution should be formed, it should be a Congress, containing a fair and adequate Representation of the Colonies, and its authority should sacredly be confined to these cases, viz. war, trade, disputes between Colony and Colony, the Post-Office, and the unappropriated lands of the Crown, as they used to be called. . . . These Colonies, under such forms of government, and in such a union, would be unconquerable by all the Monarchies of Europe.

His comment about a national government was essentially an afterthought. It would be up to the colonies to form a national constitution, if they so chose. For his part, Adams had expressed his reservation that a national constitution was necessary. Remembering that he penned several distinct letters to delegates containing his thoughts on forming governments, it is worth examining the two other extant versions of the letters with the pamphlet's proposal above. Comparing these iterations reveals the evolution of his ideas for a "Continental Constitution." In his first letter outlining his proposals on government, to William Hooper of North Carolina, he wrote:

> We have heard much, my dear sir, of a Continental Constitution—for my own Part I see no Occasion, for any but a Congress. Let every Colony please itself without Controul in its own Constitution. Let a fair and equitable Representation of every Colony, appear in Congress, and let the Authority of that great Council be Sacredly confined to three Cases, War, Trade, and Disputes between Colony and Colony.

In Adams's second letter, to John Penn, also of North Carolina, he stated:

> We have heard much of the Continental Constitution. I see no occasion for any But a Congress. Let that be made an equal and fair Representation of the Colonies, and let its Authority be confined to three Cases, War, Trade, and Controversies between Colony and Colony. If a Confederation was formed agreed on in Congress, and ratified by the Assemblies: These Colonies under such Terms of Government and such a Confederation would be unconquerable by all the Monarchies of Europe.

Taken together, these passages suggested that a national constitution, should the colonies choose to adopt one, would resemble a confederate union of colonies operating with a single national Congress, with no hint of legislative supremacy. And though he had laid out a plan for separation of powers among three distinct branches of government—legislative, executive, and judicial—and a system of checks and balances among the branches for colonial governments, there was nothing in his proposals that recommended such a scheme for the nation. The national government simply would be a confederate Congress, most likely along the lines of the present Continental Congress, with a few additional powers.

Was the new Congress to be divided along the lines that he suggested for the colonies? There was no clue, forcing the reader to leap from Adams's prescriptions for colonial government to the national government in order to make such an assumption. Were there to be checks and balances in the national government? That was not addressed. How should representation in the national Congress be determined? The only hint of an answer provided by Adams was that the Congress should have "a fair and adequate Representation of the Colonies." Would it not be reasonable then to assume that the Congress would represent the colonial assemblies directly? Though he didn't say so, there is little doubt that Adams intended for the Congress to be a creature of the colonies, arising directly out of their authority.

What Adams did explicitly mention were the constraints on the national Congress. Its powers should be limited to those expressly established when created. He gave examples: war, trade, disputes among the colonies, and authority over "unappropriated lands of the Crown." Confining Congress's authority to expressly delegated powers, likely granted by colonial governments directly, reinforced a confederate plan. And though he equated a Continental Constitution with the national Congress, he left it entirely to the colonies to decide whether such a constitution was the source of powers for the Congress. In short, he paid attention to colonial constitutional and structural principles but next to nothing to the national government. In time, *Thoughts on Government* came to be regarded as a founding document for the nation's Constitution and national government. But at this point in his thinking, Adams sketched out little more than a weak union of colonies with, surprisingly, a single-chamber national legislative body.

That the idea of a superior "continental authority" was not expressed in his pamphlet did not mean that Adams hadn't given any thought to the question of a national government. In fact, he said in 1776 that "the most intricate, the most important, the most dangerous and delicate business" would be the creation of a national government.[7] Perhaps the reason Adams said so little at this time about such a national government was that he was not ready to address the matter.

Comparing the pamphlets, there is some convergence of ideas between *Common Sense* and *Thoughts on Government*. Paine and Adams agreed, for example, on a central legislative body to replace British rule. There would be no monarch, no independent executive outside of the legislative body. And though one might reasonably infer otherwise from Adams's complex prescriptions spelled out for colonial legislatures, the national Congress was to be unicameral in structure. Adams seemingly ignored his own reservations about so simple a plan. Paine had explicitly recommended a single-assembly legislative body for the nation. Adams's sketch implicitly seemed to do the same.

Paine and Adams also agreed on some kind of national constitution. Paine used the words "charter" in his pamphlet, and he clearly called on the colonies to hold a "continental conference" for the purpose of framing a "Continental Charter, or Charter of the United Colonies." He also spelled out a scheme for how representatives should be chosen to attend this conference. For his part, Adams mentioned a "Continental Constitution," leaving the process of how it should be formed up to the colonies, and then only if they saw the necessity for it. But both men were thinking along the same lines: The creation of a national government required a national constitution that should produce a Congress to govern the nation. There were more areas of agreement.

Indisputably, Paine and Adams were both republicans and patriots. Both saw in a large country such as America the necessity of a representative form of governance. Both recommended annual elections for representatives. And for both men, "the law was king" as Paine wrote in *Common Sense* ("good government is an empire of laws" Adams wrote in *Thoughts on Government*). Proclaiming the rule of law as the ultimate authority, both regarded monarchial claims to power as illegitimate. Both, therefore, were radicals, and both could have been charged with treason for publicly expressing their views. (Paine was eventually so charged years later upon his return to England and after the publication of his treatise *Rights of Man*, which continued the development of his republicanism and was intended to undermine monarchical claims to authority. He fled to France in the nick of time to avoid being arrested.)

There was a hint of another area of agreement between Paine and Adams with respect to national powers. Adams mentioned that securing the Crown's "unappropriated lands" should be a power of the national Congress. Paine would be on board with that recommendation as it fit his own continentalist perspective. With historically ill-defined western boundaries that sometimes overlapped, several large states made claims to their frontier lands during the debates on the Articles of Confederation. Those claims eventually blew up after independence and threatened the ratification of the articles. Virginia, for example, claimed its western lands, and Maryland, a small colony with no additional westward lands to claim (its boundaries were well defined), held up the ratification process unless the dispute was settled. The small states saw no winning proposition for them, as several large states were bound to reap great value by claiming and controlling those western lands. Instead, the small states wanted the lands ceded to the new union, which might benefit everyone. It was a critical battle that almost sank the Articles of Confederation and was an early precursor of what became the large-versus-small-states conflict that engaged the Constitutional Convention in 1787. Virginia eventually capitulated, proposing that the colonies' westward lands be reserved for new states entering the union, on an equal footing with the original thirteen states. Paine published a pamphlet, *Public Good*, in 1780 addressing the dispute in which he backed up his continental vision by arguing on the side of Maryland instead of Virginia.[8] In the end, Maryland signed off on the new proposal, and the Articles of Confederation was ratified in 1781.

Finally, Paine and Adams both understood that their recommendations for governance were not fully developed plans; they were aware that their plans were not political treatises. Both saw their suggestions as offering only temporary schemes that would ultimately have to be addressed by the colonists. It bothered Adams, in particular, that his plans had been so sketchy and done in such haste. Both men in future works attempted to develop their ideas into more-coherent political thought.

While there were these areas of convergence, fundamental differences between *Common Sense* and *Thoughts on Government* outweighed areas of agreement. Paine urged Americans to declare their independence from Britain; Adams paid no attention to that subject in his pamphlet, though he didn't need to. By the time he published *Thoughts on Government*, the movement for independence in the colonies and among the people was already surging ahead and, most likely, was unstoppable. The only thing Adams could hope for was to slow it down and try to manage it.

A vital difference between the two pamphlets was Paine's proposition that colonial assemblies should be "subject to the authority of a Continental Congress." There is no hint of such power-sharing subordination in *Thoughts on Government*. Adams stated clearly that the authority of the national Congress should be "confined" to expressly delegated powers (some domestic, some foreign). Interestingly, Paine and Adams were very close in their descriptions of the authority that a national Congress should possess (war, foreign affairs, relations among the colonies, a post office, etc.), even as they disagreed about the scope of its powers. Everything prescribed by Paine in *Common Sense* portrayed him as a nationalist. His principle that "our strength is continental, not provincial," pervades his writings. A weak union of colonies could not achieve success; instead, unity was a necessity: "It is not in numbers but in unity, that our great strength lies." Paine argued that America had the numbers to build a powerful army and the materials and wealth to build a fleet. Besides, he believed America had just the right population to allow it to become "united." And only by doing so could it genuinely promote international trade, ensure domestic tranquility and security, and engage the rest of the world as an independent player in the realm of international relations. In a witty quip, Paine remarked that America would always find a market for its grain so long as "eating is the custom of Europe."

There were other differences. To say that Paine and Adams were republicans is not to say both were democrats. To Paine, "republican" and "democratic" were, practically speaking, synonyms. For his part, Adams did not equate the two terms at all. One important clue to this difference concerning representation related to their views on equality. Paine offered a hint in *Common Sense,* suggesting that representation in the colonial assemblies should be expanded to become "more equal." Adams preferred the traditional property qualifications of freemen as a basis for representation in the colonies, though he did leave those qualifications in his pamphlet up to the colonies to determine. Paine's view, as we'll see in the next chapter, prevailed in the Declaration of Independence, embodied in Jefferson's use of the terms "equal" and "people," though both terms were as ambiguous as they were sweeping.

Paine continued developing his democratic ideas over time in his writings. Adams already saw enough in *Common Sense* to be alarmed by Paine's "democratical" tendencies, and he stuck to his own traditional version of republicanism, not only in *Thoughts on Government* but throughout his life. Indeed, the patron of balance recommended balancing representation in the new governments so as to mirror society's various interests, suggesting that equal representation in fact meant that "equal interest among the people should have equal interest in it." It was Adams's subtle statement for balancing the interests within the existing social order and maintaining the status quo, a statement entirely different from Paine's conception of representation based on expanding equality. Though Paine also called for a representative system, he was willing to place greater trust in the populace; Adams preferred to "depute power from the many, to a few of the most wise and good," equating representation with classic notions of republican rule, which emphasized virtuous leadership.

Adams distrusted popular government. Acknowledging the people as the base of political authority, he nevertheless structured government to curtail their influence. And since Adams generally regarded the masses with a wary eye, he was uncomfortable with a unicameral legislative body. A single assembly could be subject to "fits of humour, starts of passion, partialities of prejudice, and consequently productive of hasty results and absurd judgments," he wrote in *Thoughts on Government*. Such an assembly could be just as tyrannical as a monarch. Paine, on the other hand, found much to admire in the nature of man; though like all classical liberals who believed that government was necessary because of moral imperfections, he did not fear a "more equal' representative assembly becoming corrupt. It was, perhaps, a difference in Paine's and Adams's religious beliefs that led to their different outlooks.

What was corrupt was not man, Paine thought, but the English government. "Deists like Paine believed that man was perfectible, with an inborn moral sense, and they substituted for the fall of man his corruption by tyrannical governments," wrote historian Eric Foner.[9] Paine, in short, believed in the potential goodness of humankind. That, of course, permitted him to advocate for a more democratic form of governance.

Adams's insistence on all the checks and counterchecking on powers built into governmental structures as prescribed in his *Thoughts on Government* was an idea Paine had ridiculed in *Common Sense* (when describing the English constitution) as an absurdity. Paine had faith in the common man, but Adams found virtue mostly among the few "wise and good." Because of Paine's more egalitarian vision of American society and his notion that humans were less likely to be corrupted, he proposed a simple government.[10] But as Adams was more circumspect about human nature, he offered explicit structural controls for those attempting to found new constitutions and governments for their colonies.

If Adams had little to say about constitutions, how they should be formed and who should form them, Paine had already said much more in *Common Sense*. A critical difference in their thinking on constitutions concerned their origin. Paine believed that a constitution is antecedent to government. "A constitution is not the act of a government, but of a people constituting a government; and government without a constitution is power without right," he wrote years later in *Rights of Man*.[11] Moreover, in *Common Sense,* Paine hinted at a doctrine he came to champion, the idea of popular sovereignty: "A charter is to be understood as a bond of solemn obligation, which the whole enters into, to support the right of every separate part, whether of religion, personal freedom, or property."

Though Adams would agree with Paine's provision that a government without a constitution is power without right, he said little about constitutions in *Thoughts on Government*. What Adams did explicitly say about a constitution was:

> A Constitution . . . introduces knowledge among the People, and inspires them with a conscious dignity, becoming a Freeman. A general emulation takes place, which causes good humour, sociability, good manners, and good morals to be general. That elevation of sentiment, inspired by such a government, makes the common people brave and enterprising. That ambition which is inspired by it makes them sober, industrious and frugal. You will find among them some elegance, perhaps, but more solidity; a little pleasure, but a great deal of business—some politeness, but more civility.

A republican constitution, then, was necessary to govern the masses and to encourage republican civility. Adams harbored no illusions that a republican government would improve human virtue; instead, a good constitution could only hope to encourage civic virtue.

The colonies had their founding charters, and Adams knew that colonial governments would have to throw them off in order to create their own new governments. There was little hint of popular sovereignty in the process; Adams assumed that colonial legislatures would create new charters, and he offered no suggestion that founding a constitution should be an act that originated from some source other than the representatives in the existing colonial governments. Paine offered a more detailed plan. Writing in *Common Sense,* as Adams had in his pamphlet, about a constitution and knowledge, Paine put the thought in an entirely different context as he detailed a plan for how a national constitution might arise:

> A committee of twenty-six members of Congress, viz. two for each colony. Two members for each house of assembly, or Provincial

> convention; and five representatives of the people at large, to be chosen in the capital city or town of each province, for, and in behalf of the whole province, by as many qualified voters as shall think proper to attend from all parts of the province for that purpose; or if more convenient, the representatives may be chosen in two or three of the most populous parts thereof. In this conference, thus assembled, will be united, the two grand principles of business, knowledge and power. The members of Congress, Assemblies, or Conventions, by having had experience in national concerns, will be able and useful counsellors, and the whole, being impowered by the people will have a truly legal authority.

To Adams, a constitution would bring knowledge to the people, serve as something of a model for civic responsibility, and guide the development of its citizens. To Paine, representatives from a diverse population founding a constitution would bring their knowledge to the process of creating the document, providing a foundation for its authority and granting it power. For Adams, law made by "wise and good" representatives who proportionally reflected the existing and competing interests in society conferred legitimate authority. For Paine, law also provided legitimate authority, but only if the system of representation was "more equal" and the constitution itself was considered to be fundamental law.

Though Adams had drawn on many features of the mixed English constitution to sketch out his own ideas of governance for the colonies, Paine would have none of that. If Adams admired the English constitution with its class-based division of powers, Paine dismissed the highly praised model and rhetorically asked, where can the English constitution be found? Implicitly, Paine rejected the view that sovereignty should be divided between the people and government. And he saw little need for a complex government arrangement with internal checks and balances. For him, the consent of the people and periodic elections were the best check against the potential abuse of traditional authority. After all, Paine insisted, the English constitution was full of internal controls within its own structure, and that had guaranteed Americans no safeguard whatsoever against British tyranny. Instead, sovereignty retained by the people and established by a properly formed constitution provided the primary means of limiting power. It was time for America to found a new constitution and create a democratic republic.

But *Common Sense* presented a constitutional plan that was far more democratic than Adams liked. For one thing, Paine had no use for English principles in an American society devoid of hereditary rights and privileges, so his constitutional thoughts do not mimic those foundational principles for a new American government. There was no reason, in his mind, why a new system of representation should preserve Old World distinctions that never applied to America. It was time to cut loose from the institutions and traditions of the past and begin to think about creating an entirely new constitutional order. Americans had it in their power to "begin the world over again." It was on this point that *Common Sense* and *Thoughts on Government* fundamentally differed.

Adams has long been given credit for creating a constitutional scheme in *Thoughts on Government* that provided the founding principles for American constitutional thought, especially for several states and the Constitution of 1787. That his scheme of balanced government—to be achieved through a separation of powers, checks and balances, and call for an independent judiciary—and his principle of the rule of law helped influence the founding of the present American Constitution is not disputed here. But for far too long, Paine's political thought as expressed in *Common Sense* (and his other writings during the American Revolutionary period) has been given little, if any, credit for germinating constitutional ideas. To this day, his pamphlet is universally acknowledged for spurring on the American independence movement, but not much else. And though Paine's ideas influenced several state constitutions being developed at the time of American independence, chiefly by his call for a single-house assembly, it is clear that Adams's proposals, in the long run, were more closely aligned with the types of governments other states developed. Even though some early state constitutions initially reflected Paine's single-house legislative model (such as Pennsylvania's), they soon abandoned that model. But what about the immediate national constitution, the one developed and ratified during the War of Independence, the Articles of Confederation? That constitution has the imprints of both Adams and Paine.

Certainly, the two men were not the first to dabble in constitutional architecture for the new American republic. The growing colonial literature of resistance from 1763 to 1775 had become increasingly revolutionary in tone as time and again, efforts at reconciliation with Britain had come to nothing. Principles of constitutionalism—limitations on powers, checks and balances, representation, and even judicial review—had been previously described in America by James Otis, John Dickinson, James Wilson, Alexander Hamilton, and John Adams, all with the thought that the defects of the English constitution could still be remedied and the conflict resolved. Few resistance writings, however, called for a declaration of independence or the creation of a brand new constitution. Paine's *Common Sense* did both. And though Adams had projected that a "union of colonies . . . and an American legislature," might be necessary in his earlier *Letters Addressed to the Inhabitants of the Colony of Massachusetts Bay*, he resisted calling for an outright abolition of English constitutional principles. Instead, Adams's proposals in *Thoughts on Government* continued to preserve essential elements of English constitutionalism. A semblance of class distinctions, property qualifications, and a classical sense of republican virtue (a select number of people should depute power to a few "wise and good" representatives to govern) informed Adams's pamphlet. His scheme retained some sort of principle of "mixed" government, even though royalty and hereditary privilege never really applied in American society. On the other hand, because of his support for unchecked popular government, Paine has been described as an advocate of "unmixed" democracy.[12]

In spite of their differing views of republicanism, the tentative principles of American constitutional thought published by Paine and Adams in their two pamphlets on the eve of American independence in 1776 influenced the formation of America's first independent governments. Taken together, their pamphlets extolled an American style of constitutionalism. A written constitution; legislative supremacy;

unicameralism or bicameralism; separation of powers and checks and balances, or a single legislative authority; competing notions of equal representation; annual elections; executive authority located within the legislature; an independent judiciary (Adams); rotation of all offices; the rule of law; constitution based on popular sovereignty (Paine); individual rights; and a division of powers between the colonies and the national government—all were principles that were debated and informed America's early constitution building.

These critical constitutional thoughts addressed, what remained was to declare independence and form a new government. The Continental Congress's retaliatory measures against England's Prohibitory Act had been an important event in moving that body toward accomplishing its first task. Adams, as a member of the Congress, had a direct hand in helping America achieve independence and form the first national constitution, the Articles of Confederation. Paine's writings influenced both achievements as well, though it took the new country some time before it began to realize the importance of his continental vision for governing America. But for now, independence was the next step.

Four

A Declaration

FIVE MONTHS BEFORE CONGRESS BEGAN THE PROCESS OF declaring independence in 1776, Thomas Paine's *Common Sense* called for a "manifesto" to be published, a "Declaration of Independence" creating "Free And Independent States of America," the first four words of which made their way into the language of Richard Henry Lee's resolution of June 7 (see below) and into the Declaration of Independence.[1] Now, in early May, with public pressure mounting for the Continental Congress to do something, John Adams sensed the time was right for Congress to take a formal stand against Great Britain.

In late April, perhaps reacting to public pressure to do something, three southern colonies—South Carolina, Georgia, and North Carolina—allowed their delegates to vote for independence. Colonial hesitation over independence was beginning to crumble.[2] Fearful that British ships of war were gathering somewhere off New England's coast to prepare for an attack, many colonists had become alarmed and were coming around to Paine's warning in *Common Sense* that "the period of debate is over." As if to underscore the concern, two

British ships bombarded defensive bulwarks in the Delaware River near Philadelphia on May 8 and 9 before finally turning away. Members of Congress could hear the cannonade.

Even though there was still resistance in Congress to taking the next step toward independence, chiefly led by John Dickinson and the Pennsylvania delegation, Adams teamed up with Richard Henry Lee to introduce a resolution on May 10 that would authorize the colonies to assume the powers of government. The resolution was unanimously approved. Whether Adams wrote the resolution is uncertain, but he wrote the preamble to it, which was introduced on May 15. The measure, for all practical purposes, formally ended any further efforts toward reconciliation and set in motion the necessary steps for Congress to declare independence:

> Whereas his Britannic Majesty, in conjunction with the lords and commons of Great Britain, has, by a late act of Parliament, excluded the inhabitants of these United Colonies from the protection of his crown; And whereas, no answer, whatever, to the humble petitions of the colonies for redress of grievances and reconciliation with Great Britain, has been or is likely to be given; but, the whole force of that kingdom, aided by foreign mercenaries, is to be exerted for the destruction of the good people of these colonies; And whereas, it appears absolutely irreconcileable to reason and good Conscience, for the people of these colonies now to take the oaths and affirmations necessary for the support of any government under the crown of Great Britain, and it is necessary that the exercise of every kind of authority under the said crown should be totally suppressed, and all the powers of government exerted, under the authority of the people of the colonies, for the preservation of internal peace, virtue, and good order, as well as for the defence of their lives, liberties, and properties, against the hostile invasions and cruel depredations of their enemies; therefore, resolved, &c.[3]

Though this resolution also passed, it did so only after heated debate, because all understood the effect of it: there would be no turning back now. A direct link between Adams's recommendation in *Thoughts on Government* that "oaths and affirmations" must be taken in the name of colonial authority and no longer the Crown, and other similar thoughts expressed in his resolution, can be observed. Of particular note was Adams's use of the phrase "lives, liberties, and properties," rights that appear, with one important variation, in the Declaration of Independence.

On May 15, the debate over independence ended. Adams believed then and from then on that his May 15 preamble was actually a formal act of independence, and he took pride and said so in his writings at the time and later, in bringing Congress to this critical point. But it took another founder to get American independence to the next step.

Thomas Jefferson was a late arrival to the Continental Congress that spring. Though Adams and Jefferson would one day have a falling out that would make them long-term political enemies (they eventually put aside their differences), they had in spring 1776 the same goal of independence and worked together in the Congress to achieve it. Not everyone, even in late May, shared their agenda, but more colonies were authorizing independence. Virginia was one of the colonies that instructed its delegates in mid-May to declare independence, and on June 7, Richard Henry Lee from that colony introduced the following resolution:

> That these United Colonies are, and of a right ought to be, free and independent states, that they are absolved from all allegiance to the British Crown, and that all political connection between them and the state of Great Britain is, and ought to be, totally dissolved.[4]

The resolution was a succinct statement of moral imperatives and a declaration of intentions. Now the die was cast, at least in words, but because some delegations—especially Pennsylvania's which also happened to be meeting upstairs in Philadelphia's statehouse where the Congress was meeting below—begged for additional time to gain support from their constituents before a vote was held, action on Lee's resolution was postponed until the end of June.

In the meantime, Congress took an important step pending the vote. A committee of five delegates, including Jefferson and Adams, was appointed to prepare a declaration of independence. The group, which soon became known as the Committee of Five, chose Jefferson to draft the document. Later in life, Adams and Jefferson offered differing accounts as to how he was selected to write the draft. Adams stated that he and Jefferson were appointed as a subcommittee to draft the document, a fact that Jefferson disputed. In any case, Jefferson soon produced a first draft of the declaration, which he shared with Adams and committee member Benjamin Franklin, who, according to Jefferson's account, made "small" editorial changes before the draft was submitted to the committee and then sent to the Congress. Some of the minor changes were noteworthy. For example, Adams substituted "self-evident" for "sacred & undeniable" in Jefferson's draft statement about truths.[5]

Jefferson wrote the first draft of the declaration alone while at his lodging on the outskirts of Philadelphia. Drawing on his knowledge of political thought and writings he likely had on hand, such as George Mason's *Virginia Declaration of Rights* and his own recent draft of a constitution for Virginia that he had been working on, he crafted the first draft of the Declaration of Independence in just a few days. Pauline Maier pointed out in her book on the declaration, *American Scripture*, that the *Pennsylvania Gazette* published Virginia's Declaration of Rights on June 12, the day after the Congress appointed the Committee of Five to draft the Declaration of Independence.[6] Over the next two weeks, Jefferson's draft underwent revisions before finally being presented by the Committee of Five to the Congress on June 28. After the Congress declared independence on July 2, and continuing until it voted to accept the document on July 4, 1776, Congress revised the committee's draft.

Like Paine, Jefferson had mastered a simple, fluid, and persuasive style of writing, often punctuated by stirring and memorable words that are easily read. Jefferson's style and opening thoughts in the Declaration of Independence are especially evocative of Paine's egalitarian and democratic vision, so much so that a few historians have argued that Paine had a direct hand in drafting the declaration. While

Jefferson was an admirer of Paine's pamphlet and writing ("No writer has exceeded Paine in ease and familiarity of style, in perspicuity of expression, happiness of elucidation, and in simple and unassuming language"), and clearly was inspired by Paine's thoughts, there is little agreement with the assertion that Paine had a direct role in composing the declaration.[7] Adams certainly had a role, albeit an editorial one, but the draft as prepared by Jefferson clearly reflects more of Paine's ideology than of Adams's more conservative views as expressed in his *Thoughts on Government.*

As presented to the Congress, the declaration reveals a preponderance of Lockean ideas—principles that were universally acknowledged among those with Whiggish political leanings.[8] The contract theory of the origin of society and political authority, a belief that legitimate power rested upon the consent of the governed, and the natural rights of life, liberty, and property were all well understood principles in eighteenth-century America and Britain. The right of revolution against a tyrannical government, especially when a contract was broken, was also recognized. Indeed, using almost exact phraseology here and there found also in John Locke's *Second Treatise on Government*, Jefferson was accused, even at the time, of copying Locke, particularly when building his case in the declaration for the right to revolt against monarchial authority. Jefferson later denied he had consulted any books or pamphlets when preparing his draft.[9]

That there is not a lot of carefully crafted or even new political thought about government in the Declaration of Independence is not surprising; that, after all, was not its purpose. Instead, the document was written to explain to Britain and to the world why the American colonies, acting in unison, were severing all ties to the British government and formally declaring war against it. And for the British audience, the declaration's announced political theory would certainly sound familiar.

Opposite: The first page of Thomas Jefferson's draft of the Declaration of Independence. Note the edits credited to Benjamin Franklin and John Adams in the left hand margin. (*Library of Congress*)

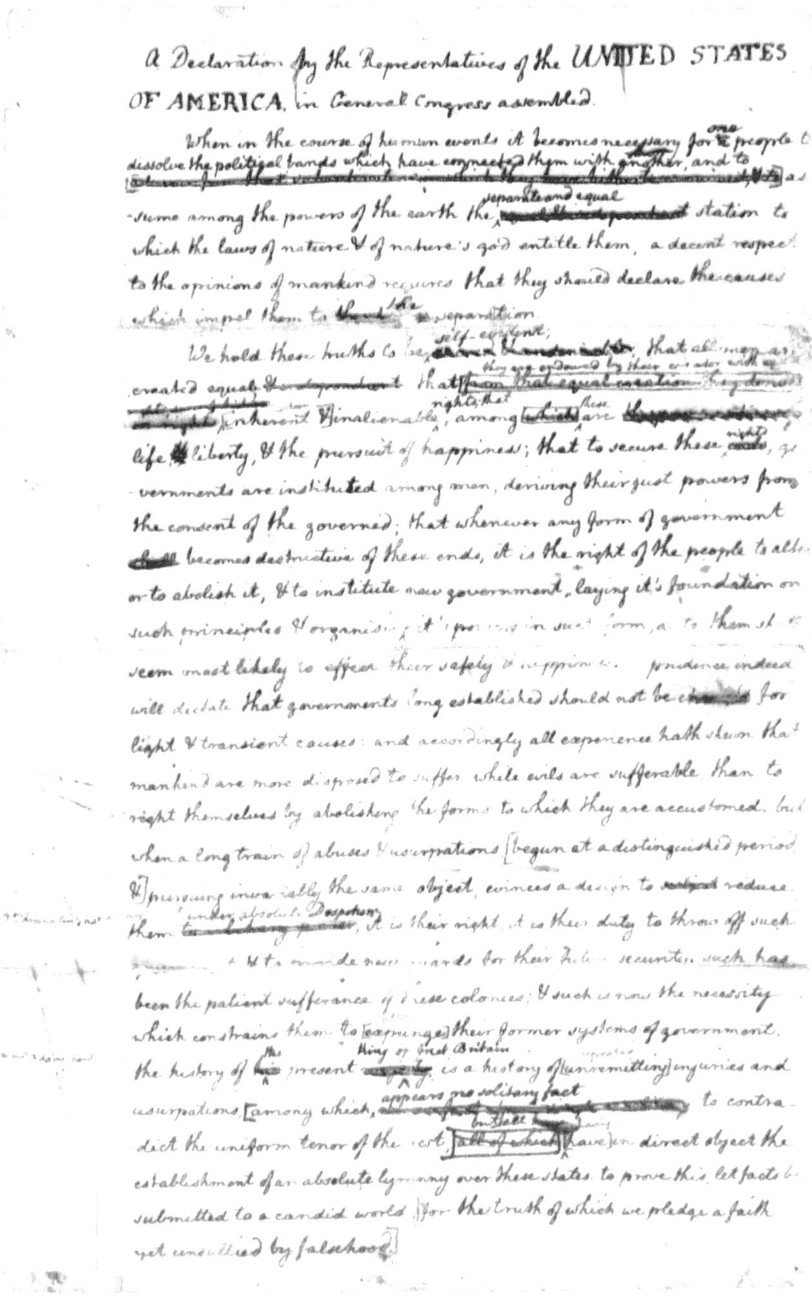

A Declaration by the Representatives of the UNITED STATES OF AMERICA, in General Congress assembled.

When in the course of human events it becomes necessary for one people to dissolve the political bands which have connected them with another, and to assume among the powers of the earth the separate and equal station to which the laws of nature & of nature's god entitle them, a decent respect to the opinions of mankind requires that they should declare the causes which impel them to the separation.

We hold these truths to be self-evident; that all men are created equal; that they are endowed by their creator with inherent & inalienable rights, that among these are life, liberty, & the pursuit of happiness; that to secure these rights, governments are instituted among men, deriving their just powers from the consent of the governed; that whenever any form of government becomes destructive of these ends, it is the right of the people to alter or to abolish it, & to institute new government, laying it's foundation on such principles & organising it's powers in such form, as to them shall seem most likely to effect their safety & happiness. prudence indeed will dictate that governments long established should not be changed for light & transient causes: and accordingly all experience hath shewn that mankind are more disposed to suffer while evils are sufferable, than to right themselves by abolishing the forms to which they are accustomed. but when a long train of abuses & usurpations [begun at a distinguished period &]pursuing invariably the same object, evinces a design to reduce them under absolute Despotism, it is their right, it is their duty to throw off such government, & to provide new guards for their future security. such has been the patient sufferance of these colonies; & such is now the necessity which constrains them to [expunge] their former systems of government. the history of the present king of Great Britain is a history of [unremitting] injuries and usurpations, [among which, appears no solitary fact to contradict the uniform tenor of the rest, but all have] in direct object the establishment of an absolute tyranny over these states. to prove this, let facts be submitted to a candid world [for the truth of which we pledge a faith yet unsullied by falsehood.]

Jefferson stated later in his life, "Neither aiming at originality of principle or sentiment, nor yet copied from any particular and previous writing, [the declaration] was intended to be an expression of the American mind, and to give to that expression the proper tone and spirit called for by the occasion."[10] But the language of his declaration not only echoed Locke, it also drew heavily from several contemporary materials he had handy, especially Mason's *Virginia Declaration of Rights*.

Indeed, one of the great strengths of Jefferson's writing style in the declaration was his ability to synthesize thoughts and ideas and present them in simple, eloquent, and memorable prose. For example, a comparison of Jefferson's famous opening lines of the second paragraph of the Declaration of Independence (the version approved by the Congress on July 4) and Mason's opening lines of his *Virginia Declaration of Rights* has often been noted. In Jefferson's words:

> We hold these truths to be self-evident, that all men are created equal, that they are endowed by their creator with certain unalienable Rights, that among these are Life, Liberty and the pursuit of Happiness. That to secure these rights, governments are instituted among Men, deriving their just powers from the consent of the governed. That whenever any Form of Government becomes destructive of these ends, it is the Right of the People to alter or to abolish it, and to institute new Government, laying its foundation on such principles and organizing its powers in such form, as to them shall seem most likely to effect their Safety and Happiness.[11]

In Mason's words:

> That all men are by nature equally free and independent, and have certain inherent rights, of which, when they enter into a state of society, they cannot by any compact deprive or divest their posterity; namely, the enjoyment of life and liberty, with the means of acquiring and possessing property, and pursuing and obtaining happiness and safety. . . .That all power is vested in, and consequently from the people. . . . That government is, or ought to be

> instituted for the common benefit, protection, and security of the people, nation, or community; of all the various modes and forms of government, that is best which is capable of producing the greatest degree of happiness and safety, as is most effectually secured against the danger of maladministration; and that when any government shall be found inadequate or contrary to these purposes, a majority of the community hath an indubitable, unalienable and indefeasible right to reform, alter or abolish it.[12]

Much has been written about the striking similarity of these passages and principles and whether Jefferson simply plagiarized his version from Mason's or some other source.[13] But at the least, a side-by-side comparison of the passages demonstrates that Jefferson's version reads much better, even if he did crib his thoughts from someone else. There's little doubt that Jefferson's style ("that felicitous, haunting cadence which is the peculiar quality of Jefferson's best writing" wrote Carl Becker)[14] resonated with the Congress and the populace; on this score, his style was much closer to Paine's than that of Mason or Adams. For his part, Adams would always be envious of Paine and Jefferson for the way each could ably express public sentiments and command attention.

But writing style is not the focus here. Instead, the declaration's political thought—and how Paine and Adams contributed to that—is the subject to which we return. The declaration has three essential parts: a proclamation of universal and equal rights, a long list of specific charges against the Crown (with an oblique reference to colonial grievances against Parliament), and a statement declaring independence that repeats the words of Lee's resolution of June 7. So powerful were Jefferson's words in the second paragraph of the declaration that little else is recognized today from the document. But a perusal of the entire piece reveals, as Paine might have put it, hints of what kind of government Americans were thinking of establishing after independence.

The famous second paragraph of the Declaration of Independence is a succinct statement of American political thought. The purpose of government, the declaration informs the reader, is to secure "unalienable" rights that all men equally hold, and that among these are the rights of "Life, Liberty and the pursuit of Happiness." Governments' powers are just only if they are derived from the "consent of the governed." No matter its form, any government that fails to achieve these ends is subject to being abolished: It is a "Right of the People" to alter or abolish such government and institute a new form, so long as its powers are "most likely to effect their Safety and Happiness." And though the people will not likely abolish a government for "light and transient causes," history had shown that after a people has suffered a "long train of abuses and usurpations" and "absolute Despotism" full of "repeated injuries and usurpations," they will "throw off such a Government" and alter their former "Systems of Government." "The history of the present King of Great Britain is a history of repeated injuries and usurpations," the paragraph concludes, alleging "an absolute Tyranny over these States" that will be proven by a list of "Facts" (charges against the king) that follows.[15]

The list reads like an indictment aimed directly at the king—some eighteen specific "He has" done-such-and-so charges offered to "prove" that King George III (he is not named) is a tyrant.[16] The declaration also has a single paragraph addressed to "our British Brethren" whose "legislature" had extended "unwarrantable jurisdiction" over the colonies. But the declaration never mentions the word "Parliament." Instead it is the monarch, not his ministers or Parliament, who is charged with ruling as a tyrant over the colonies. Finally, the declaration announces that separation from the British people has become a necessity and recasts them as "Enemies in War, in Peace Friends."

A brief comment is appropriate here before analyzing the document for principles of government. The declaration mentions states as well as colonies. It uses the term "states" at the beginning by announcing that the document represents "The Unanimous Declaration of the Thirteen United States of America." It concludes by saying the "United Colonies are, and of right ought to be Free and Independent States." Clearly, states replace colonies, but the declaration did not contemplate *the* United States of America at this time, even though "the United States of America" appears twice; instead the declaration transformed thirteen formerly dependent colonies into "free and independent states," which were said to be acting unanimously in a "united" fashion through "General Congress" for the purpose of declaring independence.[17] Though the Declaration of Independence today is regarded as one of the vital documents in the creation of the nation, nationhood was not articulated by the language used in the document. Instead, the declaration envisioned thirteen "free and independent states" that "have full Power to levy War, conclude Peace, contract Alliances, establish Commerce, and do all other Acts and Things which Independent States may of right do." Without question, the Declaration of Independence announced the creation of a confederation of independent states.

The declaration is best known for espousing universal and equal human rights. There has always been interest in what appears to be Jefferson's substitution of the word "happiness" for "property" in his famous statement about life, liberty, and the pursuit of happiness. Locke had proclaimed the natural rights of life, liberty, and property, a phrase that reappears in the US Constitution's Fifth and Fourteenth Amendments. But the word "happiness" was certainly in the air long before Jefferson penned the famous phrase. Paine used the word in *Common Sense*; Adams used the word numerous times in *Thoughts on Government*; and, most importantly, Mason used the word in his *Virginia Declaration of Rights*, language that Jefferson had nearby when drafting his declaration provisions. In fact, Mason used the phrase "pursuing and obtaining happiness and safety." Jefferson echoed Mason in the second paragraph of the declaration not only by using the phrase "pursuit of happiness" but also by linking the words "Safety and Happiness." And though Mason also included the word "property" in his statement, and Jefferson did not, it should be remembered that the natural rights Jefferson specifically mentioned—life, liberty, and pursuit of happiness—are among those "certain unalienable Rights" man has. While life, liberty, and happiness are certainly priorities in the declaration's list of rights, others, including property, exist. Jefferson had ample statements about happiness to draw on when he chose to use that word in his draft. There is little reason to suspect that Jefferson meant to exclude property as a natural right. Then again, the declaration certainly deemphasized it.

But because Americans have a tendency today to read the words in the nation's historical documents—such as the Declaration of Independence, the Constitution, and the Bill of Rights—for what they say—ignoring for the most part more than 240 years of interpretation, including Supreme Court decisions and countless attempts by historians and scholars to remind us of what those words really meant or mean—they will not find much in the declaration emphasizing property rights, or privilege, or words equating "the people" with a limited number of property holders. That freemen and freeholders were the likely individuals who would provide their consent to governments in eighteenth-century America and benefit the most, therefore, by the natural-rights philosophy espoused by Jefferson in the declaration is an understanding Jefferson needn't have stated expressly. By leaving out any reference to property and instead mentioning happiness, Jefferson struck a more universal tone than his English predecessors, whether or not we can say definitively that this was intended. Readers paid attention at the time, and they do so today.

Soon enough, Jefferson's language encouraged more and more Americans to begin to assert their natural rights, rights they believed the declaration acknowledged belong to all human beings. Because of the egalitarian spirit of the declaration, more and more Americans have come to revere it as a primary founding document for their causes. And despite what John Adams might have listed as rights had he authored the declaration (would he have simply restated the words "life, liberty and properties" as he used them in his May 15 preamble?), Jefferson's words conveyed a very "democratical" vision, a message that would be approved by the Continental Congress and that would have lasting consequences for American democracy.

Equality was a contentious issue in 1776, as it continues to be today, and it certainly was not a universally supported principle then. The word "equal" ("that powerful but ambiguous word," said Pauline Maier)[18] proved to be problematic in Jefferson's original draft of the declaration, especially within the context of his failed attempt to include language blaming the king for condoning the slave trade. The Congress excised that provision. Certainly the word "equal" is one of the most ambiguous and debatable terms in the declaration. But even as Paine had called for representation to be "more equal" in *Common Sense*, Jefferson managed to go further by elevating equality to the status of a God-given right of humankind, even if the term in fact didn't encompass slaves, women, the nonpropertied or other groups that few people at the time had any thought of including. It is the universal language of the Declaration of Independence that suggests that people everywhere can be united by a belief in equality and human rights, regardless of race, religion, economic disadvantage, or gender. Still, it's worth noting that Abigail Adams's admonishment to her husband in one of her letters "to remember the ladies" when forming a government failed to gain an endorsement by her husband or anyone else in the Continental Congress,[19] something especially noteworthy because Adams always parsed the meaning of equality within the context of society's various interests. And simply put, those without property or those considered to be property had no political interests, so were not really entitled equally to the natural rights of life, liberty, and happiness, notwithstanding Jefferson's proclamation in the declaration to the contrary. (Jefferson, of course, was a slaveholder; Adams and Paine were not.)[20]

But no right envisioned in the declaration was more important than the right to abolish a despotic government and create a new form of government—the right to choose a "government of our own," as Paine put it in *Common Sense*. It was the ultimate purpose of the Declaration of Independence to break away from the old government and declare the right to create a new one. That in order to secure human rights, "it is the Right of the People to alter or abolish [a government], and to institute new Government." It must be remembered, of course, that "the people" as used by Jefferson is another sweeping, ambiguous term. It encompassed all people, the free, unfree, patriots, loyalists, and the indifferent so far as revolution was considered. Just who among "the people" could "alter or abolish" a government remained uncertain. But like the word "equal," the word "people" carries a universal appeal.

In addition to describing human rights, the declaration's second paragraph includes several principles that informed America's new governments. Among these are that government rests on the consent of the governed, that it is the right of the people to organize governmental forms and powers on such principles as they choose, and that any government that cannot provide security and happiness for the governed, or protect human rights, may be altered or abolished whenever such a government is determined by the people to be a despotism. And though the declaration reflects many of the traditional rights and principles of eighteenth-century liberal political theory, its emphasis on "the people" as a foundation for government began to build the case for an emerging American principle, the idea of popular sovereignty.

The main body of the Declaration of Independence consists of charges ("facts") leveled against the king specifically and designed to prove that the Crown had become tyrannical with respect to exercising its powers in and against the colonies. Jefferson had already developed many of these charges for the draft constitution for Virginia he had submitted to that colony (his draft arrived too late to have much impact), and he adapted them for use in the declaration. Among the most important of these charges is that the king took numerous actions without the consent of the colonial governments and repeatedly ignored petitions (such as the Olive Branch Petition of 1775, which Adams had reluctantly signed, though he thought it to be futile) from the colonies and the Continental Congress asking the Crown to intervene on their behalf to resolve the conflict between them and the homeland.

The declaration ends by asserting independence, but it did not form a new nation. That would have to come later. Instead, the states acted in unison only by the act of declaring their independence from Britain. All other authority and powers were retained by the states by announcing "that as Free and Independent States, they have full Power to levy War, conclude Peace, contract Alliances, establish Commerce, and to do all other Acts and Things which Independent States may of right do." For the moment, the Declaration of Independence created thirteen very small nations.

In addition to declaring human rights and independence, the Second Continental Congress still had to take the steps to form a national government. So even before it finally voted to accept Richard Henry Lee's resolution for independence on July 2, a committee was appointed in mid-June to draft articles of confederation. Adams was not appointed to this committee, but his ideas, along with Paine's, contributed to building the nation's first constitution.

If Pauline Maier was correct in *American Scripture* that during the time between Paine's *Common Sense* and the Declaration of Independence many of the "declarations of independence" made in the colonies and towns in spring 1776 were the real expressions of "American minds" and inspiration for the declaration,[21] then Paine must be given credit for startling those American minds and persuading Americans to confront and accept the necessity of declaring independence. Certainly, the war had brought the colonists to the tipping point, but it was Paine who pushed many reluctant colonists over the edge and away from any remaining thoughts of reconciliation. In addition, Paine's pamphlet was responsible for alarming Adams with its democratic prescriptions for government and forcing him to collect his thoughts on government and put them down on paper, and into print. Together, Paine and Adams pressed for independence, each in his own way, and started discussions among the people and colonial assemblies about what kind of new governments America should create. But the Declaration of Independence reflects Paine and Jefferson's political thought more than that of Adams, because Paine and Jefferson were more supportive of popular government. "I am not among those who fear the people," Jefferson said later in life.[22] Neither was Paine.

While Adams held a guarded opinion of popular government, he played a critical role in bringing the Congress to a vote for the Declaration of Independence. And his political prescriptions proved, in the long run, to be more influential than Paine's as America eventually adopted Adams's more complicated arrangements of constitutional powers and structures for the Constitution of 1787. But in the short run, both men influenced the creation of the first national constitution, the Articles of Confederation. Curiously, even before it formally went into effect at the close of the Revolutionary War, Paine was already unhappy with the new constitution. And there were hints during the debates over the draft of the articles submitted to the Continental Congress that Adams also sensed an emerging problem between the states and the new nation.

Five

The All-but-Forgotten Constitution

In declaring independence, Americans could count on John Locke, James Harrington, and other figures of the Enlightenment—English and American— for inspiration as they proclaimed universal human rights and political ideals. But in creating a constitution, Americans also had Montesquieu—Charles-Louis de Secondat, Baron de La Brede et de Montesquieu, to be exact, an eighteenth-century French lawyer who, it so happens, praised the English constitution for creating the freest government in the world. John Adams noted in his diary that he had begun to read Montesquieu's *The Spirit of Laws* in 1760.[1] Jefferson honored Montesquieu's influence on American ideas by saying that "no political truth is of greater intrinsic value than that embodied in Book XI—the most precious gift the present age has received." And Hamilton, after reading Montesquieu's recommendation of confederacy for small republics, proclaimed Book XI to be "a luminous abridgement of the principle arguments in favor of the union."[2] (The title of Book XI in *The Spirit of Laws* is "Of the Laws Which Establish Political Liberty, with Regard to the Constitution.")

What Montesquieu admired most about the English constitution was its form, namely a balanced government among king, lords, and commons. The idea that legitimate political power rests on the consent of the governed was, after John Locke, commonplace among enlightened eighteenth-century political thinkers. But equally persuasive to many Americans was the view that the English constitution guaranteed the greatest amount of political freedom the modern world had yet seen. English freedom, Montesquieu declared, depended on two cardinal principles of the English constitution: the separation of powers—legislative, executive, and judicial—and the balanced and "mixed" system of social classes of monarchy, aristocracy, and democracy, respectively found in Crown, Lords, and Commons. But as noted by Bernard Bailyn in his *Ideological Origins of the American Revolution*, "The clarity of the modern assumption of a tripartite division of the functions of government into legislative, executive, and judicial powers did not exist for the colonists . . . and in any case the balance of the constitution was not expected to be the result of the symmetrical matching of social orders with powers of government." Still, the principle of mixed constitution and a balanced share of power were considered principles of "a system of consummate wisdom and policy" by colonists.[3] Only a handful of English radicals, among them Joseph Priestley, Richard Godwin, and our Thomas Paine, seriously questioned the necessity of balancing government institutions with social orders as a paramount safeguard of English freedom.[4]

John Adams was one of the founders who admired Montesquieu's analysis. While Montesquieu celebrated the English constitution for its exemplary republican principles, Paine contemptuously dismissed its most leading features as useless. Freedom, *Common Sense* instructed its readers, depended not on English constitutionalism but on the constitution of the English people. The fact that the English people were no more tyrannized than they were under the constitution was thought by Paine to be quite remarkable. And the famous notion that the separated and balanced institutions of English rule were responsible for political liberty only meant to Paine that the constitution was "exceedingly complex," making it impossible to trace to the source the responsibility for government's misdeeds. Indeed, the principle of checks and balances championed by Montesquieu was to Paine a mere absurdity. As for the "mixed" nature of the English regime of king, lords, and commons, Paine could only jeer in *Common Sense*: "Why is the constitution of England sickly, but because monarchy has poisoned the republic, the crown has engrossed the commons?"

When Virginian Richard Henry Lee introduced his resolution calling for independence in early June 1776, he also introduced two others. One authorized Congress to negotiate with foreign governments. The other called for the creation of articles of confederation. The resolutions were adopted. The Continental Congress appointed a committee to begin drafting a constitution for the new republic. The committee presented the draft constitution to Congress on July 12; it was debated for more than a year before adoption, finally being sent to the states for ratification in late 1777.

Interestingly, the first national constitution created by the Congress showed only a small amount of influence from Montesquieu. There was no balanced government with checks and balances to worry about because there was no separation of powers. As a consequence, there was nothing reminiscent of king, lords, and commons, or mixed government, because the national government consisted of a single-house legislative body only. But what did approximate Montesquieu's thought was a confederated structure, an influence John Adams specifically noted in his diary about Congress's deliberations, as delegates discussed Montesquieu's ideas of confederation and debated the articles.[5] In Book XI of *The Spirit of Laws*, Montesquieu called for a "political confederacy," an alliance of republican states for purposes of defense, which would "preserve their sovereignty."[6] His proposals were echoed even earlier than the debate over confederation. Benjamin Franklin as far back as 1767 had proposed uniting the colonies in a "*consolidating union,* by a fair and equal representation of all the parts of this empire in Parliament."[7] Equal representation of the states became one of the sticking points during the debates over the Articles of Confederation, which stretched out over a year.

But by the end of the Revolutionary War, the republic was no closer to achieving a consolidated union than it was when independence was declared. In reality, the Articles of Confederation created a union of thirteen independent and sovereign republics, a direct inheritance from the language of the Declaration of Independence ("free and independent states") and the kind of confederacy prescribed by Montesquieu. As noted by several historians, "United States of America" was a plural noun for years.[8]

For his part, Adams played a vigorous role in the debates in the Continental Congress over the provisions of the Articles of Confederation. And in one revealing debate, recorded in Jefferson's notes, Adams hinted that the sovereign state governments created by the articles needed to be joined in a stronger union: "The confederacy is to make us one individual only; it is to form us, like separate parcels of metal, into one common mass. We shall no longer retain our separate individuality, but become a single individual as to all questions submitted to the confederacy."[9] Such an amalgam was not understood to be created by the articles, however, and the debate over state sovereignty versus the powers of a central government rose to a critical level early in the next decade.

In 1776, there was no sign that Adams was bothered by the concept of a single, "unbalanced" and "unmixed" national legislative body being created by the articles. Little, if anything, from his *Thoughts on Government*, crept into the debates about the separation of powers. It was the relationship between the states and the national Congress that concerned Adams, and also the question of how the states were to be represented in Congress. To the extent that he harbored any thoughts about strengthening the powers of Congress, there is little evidence to cite, aside from his comment about "one common mass" when Congress would be acting on issues related to its delegated authority. And though he was passionate about his views of representation, desiring a proportional representation system for the delegates serving the states in Congress, as advocated by all of the large states, he lost that debate as the original proposal for equal representation—one state, one vote—prevailed in the constitution as adopted. (The size of each state's number of delegates varied between two and seven, but only one vote per state could be cast.) So a brief analysis of the Articles of Confederation and what it created in the way of national governance is in order before proceeding to examine further Adams's and Paine's influence.

Lee's resolution calling for the creation of articles of confederation was not the first time the Continental Congress considered creating a national government. Several delegates attending the First Continental Congress meeting in 1774, including John Dickinson, had urged the creation of a central government and debated Joseph Galloway's Plan of Union. (Galloway's plan was very similar to an even earlier plan, the Albany Plan of Union, championed by Franklin in 1754.) Galloway proposed:

> Is it not necessary that the trade of the empire should be regulated by some power or other? Can the empire hold together without it? No. Who shall regulate it? Shall the Legislature of Nova Scotia or Georgia regulate it? Massachusetts or Virginia? Pennsylvania or New York? It can't be pretended. Our legislative powers extend no further than the limits of our governments. Where shall it then be placed? There is the necessity that an American Legislature should be set up, or else that we should give the power to Parliament or King.[10]

Galloway's plan failed by one vote, and Galloway, following Congress's further decision to expunge his plan from the record, left the Congress, soon became a Loyalist, served as a British administrator during their occupation of Philadelphia, and moved to England. Dickinson became an ardent spokesman for reconciliation during the debates over independence in the Second Continental Congress. Even so, he was assigned to chair the committee that drafted the articles for the Congress. America eventually achieved independence, but the union of the states proved to be an elusive achievement. For now, a weak national legislature would serve as the locus of the nation; instead of the "United States," the Declaration of Independence and Articles of Confederation proclaimed that the states would be separate and disunited, with a weak central government that would serve the nation for the time being.

During the Revolutionary War, the Continental Congress continued serving as the national government, though in practice it assumed de facto the war and foreign powers that were granted to the new Congress created by the articles. The Articles of Confederation was ratified by all thirteen states in 1781, and the powers began functioning de jure in 1783, after peace was secured at the end of the war. Called the Articles of Confederation and Perpetual Union, the constitution created a "league of friendship" among the states that was destined not to live up to that description. As the states were not (and had not always been) so friendly to each other, problems were bound to arise under this confederation and for the new nation. And soon they did.

The second article of the Articles of Confederation made explicit the confederated nature of the union: "Each State retains its sovereignty, freedom and independence, and every power, jurisdiction, and right, which is not by this Confederation expressly delegated to the United States, in Congress, assembled."[11] In spite of other articles formally granting express powers to the national government, mostly in the areas of war powers and foreign affairs, Article 2 remained the crux of the problem for the union. Taken together, the Declaration of Independence and Articles of Confederation underwrote independence and the states' independent sovereignty for America. But even before the Revolutionary War was over, serious issues, especially those relating to paying for the war (especially back pay for officers and soldiers), arose to challenge the new national government.

Much has been written about the weakness of the national government created by the Articles of Confederation: the lack of a power to tax and therefore raise revenue, having instead to depend on the states' good will (and their taxes) to fund the operations of the Congress; the inability to raise a military force; the lack of real authority to back up treaties and agreements made with foreign governments; the lack of power to regulate trade among the colonies; the ability to coin money but no corresponding ability to back up its value; the inability of the Congress to address the debts of the national government, especially those associated with the Revolutionary War. All these weaknesses are true, but they are the result of a deeper flaw. The principles underlying the constitution were the real problem.

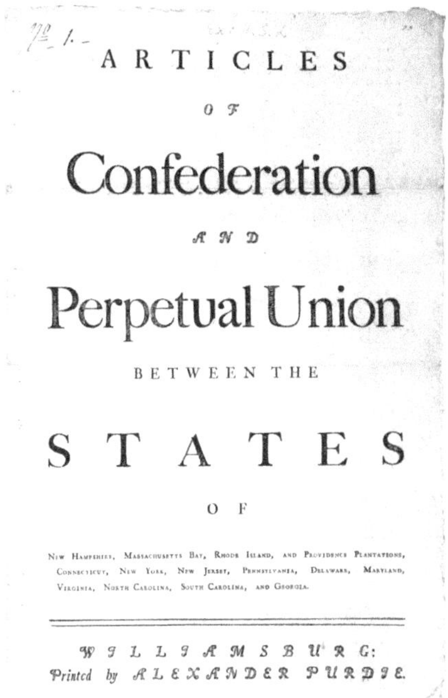

ARTICLES OF Confederation AND Perpetual Union BETWEEN THE STATES OF

New Hampshire, Massachusetts Bay, Rhode Island, and Providence Plantations, Connecticut, New York, New Jersey, Pennsylvania, Delaware, Maryland, Virginia, North Carolina, South Carolina, and Georgia.

WILLIAMSBURG: Printed by ALEXANDER PURDIE.

The title page of the Articles of Confederation. (*Library of Congress*)

Some years ago, the constitutional scholar Edward S. Corwin succinctly summarized the problem with the articles. It was the fact that they operated not on individuals but upon the states "in their corporate capacity—that, in brief, it was not a government at all, but rather the central agency of an alliance."[12] The Congress had no power to tax because it could not levy taxes on citizens. By the same reasoning, it could not enforce any of its laws, because those laws did not directly apply to people; instead, those powers lay with state legislatures, whose powers Corwin described as "excessive," and not with the national legislature. And since Article 2 made the states sovereign, independent, and free, no state could claim any authority over any other, or, theoretically, act for all of them, though some states in practice continued to obstruct other states' laws and to try to engage in foreign affairs.

It was a problem that reveals a difference in constitutional thinking between Thomas Paine and John Adams. Paine saw a "charter" or national constitution arising from the people. The national government the constitution created would operate directly on the people and be accountable to the people. Paine, in short, embraced the doctrine of popular sovereignty. Adams, on the other hand, held to the view, as expressed in his *Thoughts on Government*, that the states were sovereign and any national constitution the state legislatures formed would arise from them and be directly accountable to them. And while Adams began to sense the problem of a weak union during the debates over the draft provisions of the articles, his actions in Congress to approve the national constitution did nothing to correct the problem. A weak national government was, in fact, what he prescribed in *Thoughts on Government*.

Yet given the immediate and future problems of the articles in the continuum of things—the timeline between the articles' ratification and the ratification of the US Constitution—the Articles of Confederation served a purpose for the nascent union. They symbolized the nation, and as they expressly delegated war and foreign-policy powers to the national Congress, they formalized the location of those powers in a central authority rather than in the individual states. Above all, the articles confirmed the creation of a republican form of government for America, and in doing so forced Americans to confront the kind of republicanism that would work for a large, expanding country.

The colonists still thought in 1776 of republicanism as an alternative to monarchy and hereditary rule. The latter principles had been eliminated, at least in words, by the states' unanimous approval of the Declaration of Independence. America would now be a republican form of government, assuming it could win the war and achieve independence from British rule. But what kind of republic would it be? Reflecting classical republican thought, a republic should be a small, manageable territory that could, based on the principle of representation, govern and be accountable to its citizens. And in 1776, those small territories were states, even as they varied in size with respect to one another. Few contemplated a large, extended republic, but among those who did were Paine and Adams. How to adapt republicanism to an expanding nation was the challenge. In 1776, the two men offered different strategies.

The problems with the Articles of Confederation boiled down to two essential issues: the weak and powerless national government amounted to little more, in Corwin's words, than an "agency" of the disunited and sovereign states; and the articles placed whatever national authority they granted in a single-branch legislature with no independent executive powers. Paine and Adams agreed on several key constitutional principles for the new nation: a republican system of government based on consent, the rule of law, and a single-chamber Congress that would serve as the national government. But Adams had paid little attention to the national government or how it should be constructed in *Thoughts on Government.* His prescriptions for the nation in that pamphlet were those of a confederated republic. Even as a member of Congress and then later while serving as an emissary abroad for the new nation during the "critical period" between the Articles of Confederation and the new Constitution,[13] he showed few signs of becoming the nationalist and ardent Federalist he became by the time he joined George Washington's first administration as vice president in 1789. By that time, Adams saw the nation replace the articles with a new Constitution that embraced many of the features he had proposed for the states in his pamphlet of 1776: separation of powers and checks and balances, an executive with veto powers, an independent judiciary, and presumably an American style of mixed government reflecting the social orders of the day. But he also now found something more than a confederation. Until just before the Constitutional Convention of 1787, Adams equated federalism with confederation: a weak central government entirely accountable to independent and sovereign states. What he found on returning to America from England was a federation with significantly strengthened national powers.

By contrast, Paine from the very beginning envisioned a dual system of government with strong national powers. He neither envisioned nor prescribed a confederated republic. It was as a nation, not a group of independent states, that America would rise to hold an envious place in the world. And until America held a constitutional convention called for the purpose of creating a national constitution that both conferred and limited powers and created a dual system with a strong national government, there would not really be a "United States of America" in his mind. In the long run, it was Paine's vision that prevailed, though certainly not his model of simplicity. And though the US Constitution's structure resembled Montesquieu's and Adams's proposals regarding the tripartite arrangement of powers and checks and balances, its principles of popular sovereignty, more equal representation, and federated system of governance far more resembled Paine's initial thoughts as he had laid them out for the public in spring 1776.

Paine and Adams could each claim they got some of what they had recommended in their pamphlets for the first national constitution, the Articles of Confederation. For Paine, legislative supremacy in a federated system based in a single-house Congress was achieved. A simple plan it was indeed. There was no independent executive, no independent judiciary, and nothing that resembled a mixed government that required balancing, that is, a hierarchy of classes or privileges or social orders with a corresponding hierarchical and unequal system of representation. For Adams, whose plans for a national government were by his own admission sketchy at best in *Thoughts on Government*, the unicameral Congress was a creature of the state legislatures and rested on and was completely controlled by their authority, in his federated scheme. Indeed, Adams's ideas of a national government in his pamphlet sounded just like the recipe for the Articles of Confederation. On the whole, the new national government founded by the articles reflected in various ways the prescriptions for republican governance that had been laid out in *Common Sense* and *Thoughts on Government*.

But neither man got entirely what he wanted, either. Adams would be settled with the new arrangements of the confederation for some time, a much longer time than any of his future colleagues who would soon be called Federalists, but the articles nevertheless did not provide the constitutional controls he instinctively thought necessary to check overbearing legislative majorities. For his part, Paine soon saw, along with other nationalists, that the articles did nothing to create a strong national government. So he quickly expressed his concerns about that, even before the Articles of Confederation was ratified by all of the states. He had, after all, revealed his continentalist sentiments in *Common Sense,* and his reservations about the weakness of the articles placed him squarely among those nationalists who, from the beginning of America's founding, began to criticize the country's first constitution and started thinking about how to correct it.

Following the signing of the Declaration of Independence and during the debate over the Articles of Confederation, Adams continued serving as a delegate to the Congress and was chosen to head the Board of War and Ordnance. Late in 1777, Adams was named commissioner to France, and early the next year he sailed to France. For the next decade, he remained in Europe, with one trip home, negotiating treaties and loans and serving as minister to Great Britain for the new American government. During his brief time home, Adams drafted the Massachusetts Constitution in 1779, a document that, unlike the Articles of Confederation, embodied many of the principles of constitutional thought he had put forth in *Thoughts on Government.* The Massachusetts Constitution reflected the balanced, tripartite divisions of powers he had championed in his pamphlet and previous works, along with a bill of rights, and it proved to have legs: It is the oldest written constitution still in existence in America.

Adams finally returned to America in 1788, missing the Constitutional Convention of 1787. But even without his presence, the convention drew heavily on the principles of the Massachusetts Constitution and scheme of separated powers and checks and balances proposed in *Thoughts on Government.* The delegates to the convention had access to the first volume of a new work Adams was writing on constitutional thought while in England, *A Defence of the Constitutions of Government of the United States of America*, and acknowledged the volume's usefulness. In the first volume of his *Defence,* Adams finally admitted the faults of the Articles of Confederation:

> The former confederation of the United States was formed upon the model and example of all the confederacies, ancient and modern, in which the federal council was only a diplomatic body. . . . The magnitude of territory, the population, the wealth and commerce, and especially the rapid growth of the United States, have shown such a government to be inadequate to their wants.[14]

Adams's *Defence* had some faults of its own. According to Joseph Ellis's biography, Adams's book was "sprawling" and of "inchoate character," and "fully three quarters of the pages in the *Defence* . . . were lifted verbatim from other books, only a small portion of which were indicated by quotation marks."[15] In essence, Adams plagiarized much of the work. And this from an author, it may be remembered from chapter 1, who had accused Paine of running "about picking up what Information he could," in short, of not being an original thinker. Paine, accused by Adams and others of not being an original thinker, has nevertheless largely escaped the accusations of plagiarism that have followed Jefferson and Adams since the founding times.

After the Declaration of Independence was signed, Paine volunteered for the war effort and served as aide-de-camp in Washington's army during the early years of the conflict. He continued writing for the cause, most notably by completing thirteen *American Crisis* papers plus a few supplementary numbers, a superb series of wartime propaganda pieces written during the conflict to fire up the soldiers fighting on the front lines, denounce and ridicule Tories and British army officers, lift the spirits of the patriots, and support Washington's leadership of the Continental Army. Many of the words of the *Crisis* series are timeless ("These are the times that try men's souls . . . ") and have been broadcast and often quoted in presidential inaugural addresses, read to American troops during times of war, and included in reenactments of Revolutionary War events.[16]

In 1777, Paine was appointed, interestingly upon the recommendation of Adams, to the position of secretary of the Committee on Foreign Affairs for the Congress, a position he held until he was dismissed in 1799 for divulging in print secret congressional negotiations then taking place with the French government. (Paine's intention was to expose what he had decided was US envoy Silas Deane's war profiteering during the negotiations.)[17] In 1781, Paine joined John Laurens as his unofficial secretary on a trip to France (Congress refused to fund Paine's trip or give him any official role) to seek French financial assistance for the United States. He also worked for a while as secretary for the Pennsylvania Assembly (a state that initially adopted a single-house legislature) and also for financier Robert Morris in his efforts to get the states to contribute their fair share of money to Congress in support of the war. And in 1782, Paine published a "Letter to the Abbe Raynal," which he later considered to be one of his most important pamphlets, refuting the French writer's published account of the history of the American Revolution and trying to set the historical record straight. (Adams later gave Paine credit for correcting Raynal's history of the American Revolution.) Interestingly, Paine, moving from a nationalistic to an internationalist vision, proposed an international federation of nations, believing such an international organization might be possible given the advancement of civilization and emergence of powerful nations.[18]

At the end of the war, in 1783, Paine spent a few weeks as a guest of George Washington at his headquarters at Rocky Hill, New Jersey, and marched with the general and his troops as they entered New York City to reclaim the city from the departing British toward the end of the year.[19] In 1785, Paine received remuneration from the Congress, a grant of three thousand dollars, following personal pleas from Washington to the Congress to do something to acknowledge Paine's service to the cause. Paine also received some money from Pennsylvania and was given a confiscated Tory farm in New Rochelle, New York, by the state Assembly as a reward for his contributions. (He was denied help from the Virginia delegation, despite Washington's pleas on his behalf, because he sided with Maryland over the western frontier land claims made by Virginia during the ratification of the Articles of Confederation.) And in the same year, Paine was inducted into Philadelphia's American Philosophical Society.

In 1787, Paine, having revived his interests in natural philosophy, departed for Europe to seek sponsors for an iron bridge he had designed and intended to have built to span the Schuylkill River in

Pennsylvania, having been unsuccessful in his efforts to have the bridge built in America. His designs proved to be well received in Europe, but no iron bridges of his, other than models, were ever built there either.[20] (Someone once quipped that Paine, a builder of bridges, burned plenty of his own.) He did not return to America until 1802. But up until the moment he left for Europe, Paine continued making his public case for a more perfect union. Renewing a call he had originally made in *Common Sense*—and almost a year before the Articles of Confederation was ratified, and long before Adams finally admitted in his *Defence* that the confederation was bound to fail—Paine suggested once again that a constitutional convention should be held, this time for the purpose of trying to remedy the defects of the soon-to-be-forgotten articles. And now, as he was about to discover, he was not alone in calling for such a convention.

Six

The First Federalist?

In a letter written from Paris to Richard Price in 1785, Thomas Jefferson had this to say about constitutional problems that had emerged during the war years and after ratification of the Articles of Confederation:

> The want of power in the federal head was early perceived, and foreseen to be the flaw in our constitution which might endanger its destruction. . . . The happiness of governments like ours, wherein the people are truly the mainspring, is that they are never to be despaired of. When an evil becomes so glaring as to strike them generally, they arouse themselves, and it is redressed. . . . This truth was obvious on several occasions during the late war, and this character in our governments saved us. Calamity was our best physician. Since the peace it was observed that some nations of Europe, counting on the weakness of Congress and the little probability of a union in measure among the States, were proposing to grasp at unequal advantages in our commerce. The people are become sensible of this and you may be assured that this evil

> will be immediately addressed, and redressed radically. I doubt still whether in this moment they will enlarge those powers in Congress which are necessary to keep the peace among the States.[1]

The letter shows Jefferson's growing concern with the weaknesses of the Articles of Confederation in the mid-1780s, especially his concern for preserving the union, and his doubts that steps would be taken to remedy the problems. But it also raises an interesting question: Who foresaw the flaws in the nation's first constitution, and when?

In the founding period it wasn't always clear what terms such as "confederate," "federal," "consolidated," and "national" meant. As late as the Constitutional Convention of 1787, for example, William Paterson of New Jersey said "the idea of a national Government as contradistinguished from a federal one, never entered into [the public mind]."[2] To Paterson, "federal" meant the confederation; to his way of thinking, the nationalist plans advanced at the convention would undermine the federal system. (There are those to this day, of course, who would wholeheartedly agree with his assessment.) But those most vigorously pushing for a constitutional convention had one overarching goal in mind: strengthen the national government by granting it real powers.

As early as 1780, Alexander Hamilton, whom Joseph Ellis dubbed an "ultranationalist" in his book *American Creation*,[3] complained in a letter written to James Duane, a delegate to the Continental Congress from New York, about the "want of power in Congress." This, a year before the articles were ratified. He was particularly concerned about war powers, foreign affairs, finance and trade, and the necessity for Congress to be supreme in exercising power in these areas. He advocated single ministers for these functions instead of congressional boards: "There is always more decision, more dispatch, more secrecy, more responsibility where single men than when bodies are concerned. By a plan of this kind, we should blend the advantages of a monarchy and of a republic in a happy and beneficial union." Thus, Hamilton laid out his proposals to strengthen the articles in his letter to Duane:

> The Convention should assemble the first of November next [1781]. The sooner the better. Our disorders are too violent to admit of a common or lingering remedy. The reasons for which I require them to be vested with plenipotentiary authority are that the business may suffer no delay. . . . A Convention may agree upon a Confederation; the States, individually, hardly will. . . . Congress should have complete sovereignty in all that relates to war, peace, trade, finance, and to the management of foreign affairs. . . . The Confederation should provide certain perpetual revenues, productive and easy of collection; a land tax, pool tax, or the like, which, together with the duties on trade, and the unlocated lands, would give Congress a substantial existence.[4]

Note that Hamilton used the term "Confederation" while proposing much stronger powers for the central government. Within a year, there was a change of terms, as he published a series of articles titled *The Continentalist* in which he continued his argument for a strong national government, this time calling for a federal republic:

> There is something noble and magnificent in the perspective of a great Federal Republic, closely linked in the pursuit of a common interest, tranquil and prosperous at home, respectable abroad; but there is something proportionally diminutive and contemptible in the prospect of a number of petty States, with the appearance only of union, jarring, jealous, and perverse, without any determined direction, fluctuating and unhappy at home, weak and insignificant by their dissentions in the eyes of other nations.[5]

Many authors have agreed that Hamilton was the first person to recommend that a convention be called to revise the Articles of Confederation: "Seven years before the Constitutional Convention, Alexander Hamilton became the first person to propose such a plenary gathering," wrote Ron Chernow.[6] But as we'll see, Hamilton was not the first person to call for a constitutional convention. And he was not the first one to publicly call for such a meeting to revisit the Articles of Confederation.

Not too long after Hamilton's letter, George Washington, before he relinquished power as commander of the Continental Army, issued a "Circular Letter to the States" imploring them to strengthen the powers of the union: "It is indispensable to the happiness of the individual States, that there should be lodged somewhere, a Supreme Power to regulate and govern the general concerns of the Confederated Republic." He wanted a continental army, taxing power for Congress, and a way to pay unpaid troops and cover debts. Making his appeal to the "citizens of America," Washington called for "An indissoluble Union of the States under one Federal Head."[7] Washington now used the term "federal" also. Washington's frustrations with Congress's inability to support the war had made him a nationalist.

Thomas Paine knew all too well of those frustrations. Serving for a time in Washington's army as aide-de-camp to General Nathanael Greene, Paine saw firsthand the difficulties Washington had procuring supplies, paying the troops, and keeping the army and various state militias together during the war. But Paine, of course, had expressed nationalist views from the start, though there is not in any of his writings the support expressed by a few nationalists, in particular Hamilton, for a unitar system. Paine did not attend the Philadelphia Convention of 1787; as previously noted, he had left America for Europe by the time the convention convened. But there is plenty of evidence to show that he would have cast his lot with the Federalists, as they came to be known, had he the chance. And he essentially said so. In one of his letters "To the Citizens of the United States," written after Paine returned to America in 1802, he said:

> If, then, by *Federalist* is to be understood one who was for cementing the Union by a general government operating equally over all the states, in all matters that embraced the common interest, and to which the authority of the States severally was not adequate, for no one State can make laws to bind another; if, I say, by a *Federalist* is meant a person of this description . . . *I ought to stand first on the list of Federalists.*[8]

Presidents George Washington, Thomas Jefferson, James Madison, and John Adams. Washington and Adams were Federalists, while Jefferson was a staunch Republican. Madison, once a Federalist, switched sides and became a Republican in the 1790s. (*Library of Congress*)

Interestingly, by the time Paine wrote these words, he had come to oppose the Federalists, the party of Washington, Adams, Hamilton, and other nationalists, including James Madison, who had first come together at the Constitutional Convention to advance and then defend the Constitution and a strong national government. Paine, like Jefferson, and Madison, the "father" of the Constitution, had concluded that the Federalist political agenda that emerged during the Washington and Adams presidential administrations of the 1790s was a threat to the republic. But a decade before, Paine had indeed helped pave the way for the Federalist perspective.

His call for a "continental conference" to frame a "Continental Charter" in *Common Sense* came several years before Hamilton and Washington began to demand strengthening the Articles of Confederation. And while Hamilton and Washington struggled to find a way to create, in Washington's words, a "Supreme Power" to govern the "States under one Federal Head," neither offered much in the way of details at the time as to how that might be accomplished. Paine on the other hand spelled out in some detail how the constitutional conference might be selected and composed. And he made it clear that a legitimate national government can only arise out of the people or, more specifically, from a representative body chosen for that purpose. Government should not beget government, something that Hamilton, Washington, and Adams had not yet articulated. Paine proposed that a dual system of government, local and national, be established, and he left no doubt that only a national constitution (a "charter" as he called it then), could establish the basis of representation and create the powers of national and state legislatures. As *Common Sense* pointedly stated, "our strength is continental, not provincial."

Of course, the first national constitution, the Articles of Confederation—the one that did not last very long and was soon pushed aside—had not come about in the way Paine recommended in *Common Sense*. It was drafted and adopted by the national Congress and sent out to be ratified by the state legislatures. Government had, indeed, begat government. And as approved, the articles reflected few of the ideas put forth in *Common Sense*, save Paine's proposal for a single-house national legislature with no independent executive, judiciary, or any need for checks and balances, an idea Paine abhorred in his pamphlet. There was certainly no hint in the articles for a strong national government; in fact, there was little that could even be associated with the idea of dual sovereignty—a division of sovereign powers between the national government and the states, an idea that began to emerge only after the Constitution of 1787. That the articles needed strengthening, though, was certainly as clear to Paine as it was to Hamilton and Washington before the Revolutionary War ended. And he had numerous opportunities to make his case public during this time.

Like Hamilton, Paine thought the most striking weakness of the Congress under the Articles of Confederation was its inability to raise revenue or borrow funds to finance its operations and prosecute the war. In a special *Crisis* paper issued in October 1780, *The Crisis Extraordinary*, Paine issued a plea for the states to pay their fair share of the war costs and argued that a stronger central government was necessary.[9] He specifically recommended that Congress should have the power to lay and collect a duty on imports, a tax compatible with the kind Hamilton advocated.

Paine also supported a national bank, something Hamilton is famous for first proposing. Comparing their words about the role of such a bank is interesting. As early as 1779, Hamilton wrote that "a national bank . . . will be powerful cement to our union." And in a letter to Robert Morris, Congress's Philadelphia financier for the war and the person who unofficially established the first national bank, Hamilton wrote, "A national debt, if not excessive, will be to us a national blessing. . . . It will be a powerful cement of our union."[10] Paine had already expressed the identical thought in *Common Sense* by arguing that "a national debt is a national bond." Both founders wanted Congress to have the power to tax and to borrow in order to carry out its responsibilities for governing the nation. And both felt a national debt was worthwhile for helping create national unity.

Hamilton was also not alone in suggesting that Congress, not the states, should assume responsibility for overseeing America's "unlocated lands." In December 1780, Paine published a pamphlet titled *Public Good* that addressed Virginia's and several other states' claims to their poorly defined western boundaries. That this pamphlet rattled the members of Virginia's elite became apparent some years later when, as noted in a previous chapter, several Virginia delegates in the legislature refused to support efforts, led by George Washington, to find some remuneration for Paine for his role in bringing about independence and supporting the Revolutionary cause. Virginia and other large states had, after all, relinquished their claims to their frontier lands in order for Maryland to agree finally to ratify the Articles of Confederation. But Virginia remained unhappy about it, and especially Paine's public posture in the affair.

But the most important part of *Public Good* was Paine's call for a constitutional convention to strengthen the national government under the Articles of Confederation. Here's what Paine said:

> I shall in this place take the opportunity of renewing a hint which I formerly threw out in the pamphlet *Common Sense*, and which the several states will, sooner or later, see the convenience if not the necessity of adopting, which is, that of electing a Continental convention, for the purpose of forming a Continental constitution, defining and describing the powers and authority of Congress. . . . Those of entering into treaties, and making peace, they naturally possess, in behalf of the states, for their separate as well as their united good, but the internal control and dictatorial powers of Congress are not sufficiently defined, and appear to be too much in some cases and too little in others; and therefore, to have them marked out legally will give additional energy to the whole and a new confidence to the several parts.[11]

Paine's call in *Public Good* for strengthening the national Congress, and more clearly defining its powers, was nothing unexpected. Publicly, on numerous occasions, from *Common Sense* forward and well into the 1780s, he continued to make the case for a strong central government. When Cato had publicly attacked Paine's *Common Sense* in spring 1776, arguing for reconciliation with Great Britain, Paine responded with a series of pieces in the press known as the *Forester Letters*. The "Forester," a pseudonym Paine had used before in England, was characteristically nationalist ("the great business of the day is Continental").[12] And in his *Crisis Papers*, published from the end of 1776 to the end of the Revolutionary War, Paine consistently invoked the image of a nation and not just a collection of colonies engaged in war.

In *Crisis 2,* written at the beginning of 1777, after the Battles of Trenton and Princeton, Paine warned Lord Richard Howe, vice admiral of the British fleet and brother of William Howe, the British commander in America, that "'*The* UNITED STATES *of* AMERICA,' will sound as pompously in the world or in history, as 'the kingdom of Great Britain.'"[13] And in *Crisis 10*, published in 1782, Paine again addressed the need to strengthen the central government:

"Each state is to the United States what each individual is to the state he lives in. And it is on this grand point, our happiness as a people, and our safety as individuals, depend." Reminding patriots that the union was too weak, that it was not just a bond of "common interest and affection, he argued that the union was also a "duty of legal obligation. . . . When a multitude, extended, or rather scattered, over a continent in the manner we were, mutually agree to form one common centre whereon the whole shall move to accomplish a particular purpose, all parts must act together and alike, or act not at all, and a stoppage in any one is a stoppage of the whole."[14]

Shifting to a more challenging concern in *Crisis 10*, Paine addressed the dreaded subject of taxes and the need for the states to pay their quotas of tax revenue to Congress. Simply put, he said, without revenue, Congress could not finance the war. Returning to an idea he had floated in his *Crisis Extraordinary* of 1780, Paine proposed that people in the states would perhaps be more inclined to pay taxes if domestic and war expenses were distinct. The separate states instead might "lay taxes for raising their quotas of money, for the United States, separate from those laid for their own particular use." But noting two years later in *Crisis 10* that there were now efforts in the states to lower taxes, Paine had this to say, something that surely stands out in defense of taxes, in his times and in ours:

> When we think or talk about taxes, we ought to recollect that we lie down in peace and sleep in safety; that we can follow our farms or stores or other occupations, in prosperous tranquility; and that these inestimable blessings are procured to us by the taxes we pay. In this view, our taxes are properly our insurance money; that are what we pay to be made safe, and, in strict policy, are the best money we can lay out.[15]

But taxes continued to vex the confederation as they had from the beginning of the conflict with Britain. In 1781, Congress proposed a duty on imports (as Paine had anticipated it might do in *Public Good*), the proceeds to go to the war. Under the Articles of Confederation, unanimous consent of the thirteen states was necessary for the proposed 5 percent duty to become law. All states but Rhode Island agreed or promised to agree to the measure. Paine wrote "Six Letters to Rhode Island" in an effort to push the state into agreement. The effort failed, but in the second letter, Paine offered a key understanding of federalism: that citizenship was a matter for the nation and states: "Every man in America stands in a two-fold order of citizenship. He is a citizen of the state he lives in, and of the United States; and without justly and truly supporting his citizenship in the latter, he will inevitably sacrifice the former." And in the same letter, Paine addressed another issue of federalism, that of sovereignty:

> What would the sovereignty of any one individual state be, if left to itself, to contend with a foreign power? It is on our united sovereignty, that our greatness and safety, and the security of our foreign commerce, rest. This united sovereignty then must be something more than a name, and requires to be as completely organized for the line it is to act in as that of any individual state, and, if anything, more so, because more depends upon it.[16]

In the last-numbered *Crisis 13* at the end of the war, published on April 19, 1783, the anniversary of Lexington and Concord, Paine declared, "The times that tried men's souls" were over. He resumed his case for "the necessity of strengthening that happy union." Tying his remarks directly to passages from *Common Sense*, he reminded his readers that it is "the UNION OF THE STATES" by which Americans will be known to the rest of Europe and the world:

> The division of the empire into states is for our own convenience, but abroad this distinction ceases. The affairs of each state are local. They can go no further than to itself. . . . In short, we have no other national sovereignty than as United States. . . . Our citizenship in the United States is our national character. Our citizenship in any particular state is only our local distinction. By the latter we are known at home, by the former to the world. Our great title is AMERICANS—our inferior one varies with the place.[17]

At the end of 1783, Paine published one final, unnumbered *Crisis*, *A Supernumerary Crisis,* which summed up his thoughts for a stronger union. Noting that the nation really had no national system of commerce now that the war was over, and that the states had always struggled to pay their quotas in support of the war, Paine reminded Americans that problems with the union had to be resolved:

> United, [America] is formidable, and that with the least possible charge a nation can be so; separated, she is a medley of individual nothings, subject to the sport of foreign nations. . . . But it is only by acting in union, that the usurpations of foreign nations on the freedom of trade can be counteracted, and security extended to the commerce of America. And when we view the flag, which to the eye is beautiful, and to contemplate its rise and origin inspires a sensation of sublime delight, our national honor must unite with our interest to prevent injury to the one, or insult to the other.[18]

Paine increasingly turned his attention to strengthening the union by focusing on commerce and trade, and the inability of Congress under the Articles of Confederation to meet these new challenges. That he devoted so much attention to commerce, banking, money, and economic interests of the new nation has vexed some of his followers ever since, especially those who see Paine best through their left eye, and especially because left-leaning Paineites regard him as a champion of the working class and poor, and not a defender of elites and their monetary interests. They note, correctly, that Paine soon promoted the establishment of welfare-state features for nations in his later writings, especially in his pamphlet *Agrarian Justice.*[19] So the assumption that has often been made that the writer of *Common Sense* was a conservative on economic matters is perplexing for some.

The crux of the assumption rests on principles stated unequivocally in the opening passages of that pamphlet that the best government is that which governs least and with the least amount of expense. Moreover, scholars like to remind us that *Common Sense* and Adam Smith's *Wealth of Nations* appeared in the same year, that the two works have much in common, and that their ideas share some theoretical assumptions. Because Paine did argue that government ought to secure, among other things, property rights, some scholars have tried to temper his later radicalism by suggesting that the adjective "bourgeois" be placed before "radical."[20] But as Paine made clear in *Common Sense*, commerce and trade are among the primary objects of any nation. And as he saw it, the inability of Congress under the articles to tax and raise revenue put America at a disadvantage in the world marketplace. "Trade is not local property," he had written in "Six Letters to Rhode Island, "but belongs to all the citizens of America, without distinction of place or state."[21]

Therefore, there are good reasons why a national bank, money, and credit were important to Paine during the critical years of the Articles of Confederation's short reign. To him, a national bank was a symbol of an independent and strong nation. He wanted America to stand as an equal in world affairs and international trade and commerce. Only as a nation could it do so. And because Paine equated a strong central government with national security and the potential for achieving individual liberty and equality, he expressed many of the same sentiments that aligned him with Federalists emerging during this period, those who soon sought not to strengthen the Congress under the articles but to replace the existing constitution. Paine's hope was that commercial success and economic prosperity would come to all in America. His belief in union and economic strength was, in his mind, entirely compatible with his egalitarianism.

In 1786, Paine published his last important pamphlet before departing for Europe for a fifteen-year stay. The piece was triggered by challenges from rural Pennsylvania farmers—who controlled the Pennsylvania Assembly—to Robert Morris's Bank of North America, a bank that Paine supported from the beginning of its founding in 1781. The issue was paper money. The farmers feared that the bank would not accept the paper money they had managed to get authorized by the Pennsylvania Assembly. Fearful that Morris's bank would not honor paper money on par with specie, as the bank's notes were, the rural delegates managed to get the assembly to revoke the bank's charter. (Subsequent legislative elections ensured that the charter was restored.) Paine sided with the bank, so the farmers decided he had deserted the common people and was instead a hired pen for the wealthy mercantile and banking elites of Philadelphia. There is no evidence that Paine was a hireling (though he had once worked for the bank's founder, Morris), but he felt compelled to defend his support for the bank in a pamphlet titled *Dissertation on Government; the affairs of the Bank; and Paper Money*. The bigger struggle, Philip Foner argued in his introduction to the pamphlet in his *Complete Writings of Thomas Paine*, was between debtors and creditors. It was the kind of struggle, of course, that triggered Shay's Rebellion and further alarmed the nationalists.[22]

Aside from the particular issue of the bank's charter, *Dissertation on Government* demonstrated Paine's evolving, even maturing, thinking on several key constitutional issues: checks and balances, and the single-chamber legislature. He sensed a problem with his model of simplicity. Always believing that the people were the best repository of sovereign authority ("in republics, such as those established in America, the sovereign power . . . remains in the people") and that a written constitution was the best safeguard against the abuse of power, Paine nevertheless expressed reservations in the pamphlet about unchecked popular government for the first time. He hinted at the problem of an overbearing majority in the legislative body, writing that "despotism may be more effectually acted by many over the few, than by one man over many."[23] It was just the kind of fear Adams had expressed years earlier.

Reacting to the rise of parties in American politics, particularly the backcountry "Constitutionalists" of Pennsylvania who controlled the single-chamber assembly and acted to revoke Morris's bank's charter, Paine was forced to consider, just as Madison did later in his *Federalist No. 10*,[24] the possibility of a factious majority tyranny:

> My idea of a single legislature was always founded on a hope, that whatever personal parties there might be in the state, they would all unite and agree in the general principles of good government—that these party differences would be dropped at the threshold of the state house, and that the public good, or the good of the

> whole, would be the governing principle of the legislature within it. . . . Party dispute, taken on this ground, would only be, who should have the honor of making the laws; not what the laws should be. But when party operates to produce party laws, a single house is a single person, and subject to the haste, rashness and passion of individual sovereignty. At least, it is an aristocracy.[25]

Though Paine seemed to hint in this passage that a two-house legislative model with internal checks and balances might indeed help guard against the tyranny of an overbearing majority, exactly the kind of solution Adams had advocated, he continued to prefer the single-chamber model in later writings. Because he detested the classic system of mixed government—monarchic, aristocratic, and democratic—and especially the ideas of an independent executive and upper legislative chamber, he never really embraced the tripartite model of separation of powers and checks and balances that the Federalists came to champion.

But recognizing the potential negative effects of factions and parties in a popular government, Paine had begun to think about how to control them. Clearly, he recognized a problem, perhaps a contradiction, between his notion that people were not saints and unchecked popular rule.[26] But as Paine understood the functional separation of powers and the necessity of deputing authority, even in a unicameral system such as originally established in Pennsylvania, he rejected the checks-and-balances model in principle, the model Adams had prescribed from the beginning. And though he saw the need for some mechanism to check popular control of the single legislative system, an independent executive with veto powers over the legislature was not his solution. Instead, Paine believed that a written constitution that was genuinely amendable (the Articles of Confederation required a unanimous vote of all thirteen states and was never amended) and periodic elections were the key safeguards for maintaining free government.

As the bank dispute in Pennsylvania tested Paine's belief in simple government and the fundamental character of the American people, and he saw the need for protecting the constitution against arbitrary attempts to undermine or change it by simple majority rule and legislative action, he began to think deeply about fundamental law and the role of the judiciary. Since Pennsylvania had acted to repeal the bank charter by passing a law that would overturn it, Paine probed contract law and the role of the courts in *Dissertation on Government*:

> For admitting a question of law to arise, whether the charter, which that act attempts to repeal, is a law of the land in the manner which laws of universal operations are, or of the nature of a contract made between the public and the bank . . . the repealing act does not and cannot decide the question, because it is the repealing act that makes the question, and its own fate is involved in the decision. It is a question of law and not a question of legislation, and must be decided on in a court of justice and not by a house of assembly.[27]

Though he had not mentioned an independent judiciary in *Common Sense* (like the executive, Paine regarded the judiciary as a subordinate function of the legislature), he foresaw, if not quite the doctrine of judicial review, the necessity for the courts to step in on occasion to mediate a dispute between a charter, which he considered fundamental law, and subsequent politically motivated action to revoke it. Paine understood that there was a difference between ordinary legislation and a constitution (in this case, a charter), which was a higher law, the "law of the land."[28] And as Pennsylvania had originally granted Morris's bank a perpetual charter, Paine argued that once that was done, mere legislation could not be passed to revoke it, for the charter superseded such legislation. Thirty years later, Chief Justice John Marshall echoed Paine's reasoning in *Dartmouth College v. Woodward*, 17 U.S. 518 (1819).

Because Paine, like Jefferson, believed that nothing in governance should be done in perpetuity, several scholars have noted that "Paine on popular sovereignty did not get along easily with Paine on charter contracts."[29] It is true that Paine believed that each generation should rule for itself, that no generation should bind future generations:

"Every age and generation must be as free to act for itself, in all cases, as the ages and generation which preceded it. The vanity and presumption of governing beyond the grave is the most ridiculous and insolent of all tyrannies."[30] Still, as Paine distinguished between fundamental law, such as that of a constitution or charter, and ordinary legislation, which could change ordinarily, he outlined a scheme in *Dissertations on Government* for a periodic review of constitutions so that each generation could preserve for itself or toss out previously established constitutional provisions as it saw fit. For Paine, the principle of constitutional renewal was a key understanding of popular sovereignty, upon which all legitimate constitutions rest.

It's clear that from the beginning in *Common Sense,* Paine contributed to the development of American constitutional thought. "The publication of Paine's *Common Sense* in January 1776," stated scholar M. J. C. Vile, "heralded the rejection of the old theory of constitutionalism and opened a period of intense constitutional development in which all that was considered bad in the old forms would be discarded, and all that was considered good would be scrutinized and modified to suit the needs of an independent America."[31] Paine's writings consistently supported the idea of creating a dual form of government with strong national powers from the beginning and throughout the critical period leading up to the ratification of the new Constitution.

John Adams had to feel very satisfied with the Constitution he found upon his return to America from England a year after the Constitutional Convention and just a few months before the document was ratified. For one thing, Adams's principles of separation of powers and checks and balances, and his notions of balanced government—all ideas he had floated in his pamphlet *Thoughts on Government*—were embedded now in the new Constitution. There was even an American version of mixed government, in the form of an upper legislative chamber, the Senate. And though the new Constitution was missing a list of rights, something Adams and Paine had advocated in their pamphlets of 1776, Adams learned that a promise had been made for such a provision in the near future, through the Constitution's amendment process. It was a promise James Madison pushed to fulfillment.

Though Adams did not really adopt the Federalist position for strengthening the national government until just before the Constitutional Convention in 1787, upon his return to America he became an ardent Federalist, serving as the first vice president of the United States and as its second president, as the titular head of the Federalist Party. But Adams never embraced the egalitarian politics that began to arise during the first Federalist administrations and that ultimately came to challenge the Federalist Party in the form of Jeffersonian Republicans. He remained an elitist to the end and clung to his traditional views of mixed and balanced government. In doing so, remarked Gordon Wood, "Adams steadily isolated himself from the main line of American intellectual development."[32] It is fair to say, though, that Thomas Paine's writings had something to do with continuing the intellectual development of egalitarianism and a rising democratic tide.

As he left for Europe at age fifty on the eve of the Constitutional Convention in spring 1787, Paine must have sensed some accomplishment, knowing his call made over a decade earlier in *Common Sense* for a "Continental Conference" to frame a "Continental Charter" was finally coming to pass. He had come to America, joined its revolution, spurred its populace toward declaring independence, and helped it win the war. Now, as he left for Europe and, as it turned out, another revolution, this time in France, he knew he had put forth some essential ideas for creating a democratic republic, and a more perfect union.

EPILOGUE

In the wee hours of a crisp fall morning in 1819, Thomas Paine departed America for the last time. He was on his way home to the country of his birth, though he couldn't have known that or even, for that matter, that he was about to embark on an endless journey. After all, Paine had been dead for some time now. His funeral, held ten years before on his farm in New Rochelle, New York (because no cemetery would accept his remains), was attended by six people. Which is another way of saying that the famous revolutionary's passing was unremarkable and irrelevant, or, more likely, deliberately ignored. Paine stated in his will he hoped to rest in peace, but it was not to be.[1]

Upon his return to America in 1802, and after a long hiatus in Europe during which time he had managed to escape from England after charges of treason had been leveled against him for his revolutionary ideas in his *Rights of Man* and had been imprisoned in France for his revolutionary activities in that country (this time for not being radical enough), Paine arrived in his adopted country essentially persona non grata. Two reasons account for this disappointing reception.

One, while in France, Paine had written a critique of institutionalized religion, especially Christianity, in a two-volume work, *The*

Age of Reason. Because he attacked the doctrine of divine revelation and other fundamental beliefs of the faithful, the publication cost him the friendship of many of his old Revolutionary-era compatriots, such as Samuel Adams, who called Paine an infidel. The label stuck.[2]

Two, blaming President Washington for not doing anything to help him while he was imprisoned by the French regime during the country's bloody Reign of Terror (he barely escaped the guillotine of Robespierre), Paine published a letter attacking Washington's indifference to his plight.[3] The new US minister to France, James Monroe, eventually secured Paine's release and nursed Paine back to health after he was held in the Luxembourg prison. Monroe cautioned him against publishing his letter about Washington, but Paine went ahead with his scathing attack anyway and sent the letter to the American press, a decision that further alienated him from the American public. For his part, Washington never answered the letter. It was the end of a long friendship.

So Paine's arrival a few years later in America was mostly denounced, even by President Jefferson's daughters, who implored their father to have nothing more to do with the repudiated radical.[4] Jefferson had sent a ship to France to pick up Paine—he eventually returned on a different vessel—and initially welcomed his return, wining and dining his revolutionary compatriot. (The Federalist press had a great time chastising President Jefferson for this.) But in time, even Jefferson distanced himself from his old friend, going so far as to prohibit the publication of his correspondence with Paine during the rest of his life.[5] In his final years, Paine continued to write—mostly letters, occasional essays, and quite a few newspaper articles denouncing the Federalist Party and press—until he died in obscurity.

Now, a decade later, he was on his way back to England, forever removed from the country where he found fame in the first place. One of the former adversaries with whom Paine had feuded publicly in the press had developed second thoughts about Paine and his legacy. William Cobbett, a British pamphleteer and on-again, off-again resident of America, had changed his politics and lately come to regard Paine as an American hero. If Americans wouldn't honor Paine, Cobbett reasoned, surely the English would. So Cobbett, his son, and a hired hand went to Paine's grave on his farm in New Rochelle, dug up his body before dawn one morning, and—barely beating local officials who were alerted to the activity—absconded with the corpse and put it on a ship back to England for a proper burial and to build a monument to his legacy. Of the few American newspapers that found Cobbett's bizarre deed and Paine's final departure noteworthy, most summed up their reactions in two words: good riddance.

Back in England, Cobbett's efforts did nothing to rescue his hero's reputation. If anything, Paine's resurrection was strange and the sight of his remains disgusting to those who saw them. Cobbett never achieved his goals. An auctioneer liquidating Cobbett's estate after his death years later refused to sell the box of bones Cobbett had kept, so as the macabre contents began to be passed down through various hands over time, the bones started to disappear, a few here, a few there. Those critics in England as well as in America who had a bone to pick with Tom Paine and his radical and unorthodox ideas found all of this delightful. To them, his reputation was continuing to come apart as fast as the rest of him. Soon, Paine was simply lost. A popular nursery rhyme that arose in England at the time said it all:

> Poor Tom Paine! There he lies:
> Nobody laughs and nobody cries
> Where he has gone or where he fares
> Nobody knows and nobody cares

But the debate that Thomas Paine started with John Adams in 1776 lives on, because the differences between the two rivals reveal a fundamental question in American political thought: whether the character of the American people can be trusted to produce good government and guard against the potential abuse of power, or whether internal controls on government, such as separation of powers and checks and counterchecking, are constitutionally sufficient to ensure limited government and protect against overbearing popular movements in a democratic republic. In one sense, Adams won the debate a long time ago, for many of the Constitution's principles that reflect his views continue to hold to this day, at least in their theoretical forms. On the other hand, Paine's prescriptions for popular sovereignty and "more equal" representation—ideas Adams always thought were too "democratical"—as well as his early call for a federal republic, an idea Adams only accepted belatedly, left their mark on the US Constitution.

In a letter to his son Charles, John Adams expressed his belief that "the time will come, when more Men will think as I do than as he [Paine] does." But he also believed that he would "never be so popular as Tom Paine."[6] Adams was right about what others would come to think but wrong about his own popularity, though there has been resurgence in recent years in Paine's.

In the end, Paine's contributions to American political thought and to its evolving democratic society were of lasting value in spite of Adams's efforts to dismiss them. As for his legacy, perhaps Paine's biographer Moncure Daniel Conway put it best: "As to his bones, no man knows the place of their rest to this day. His principles rest not."[7]

Appendix A

Common Sense

Thomas Paine

1776 (Abridged)

ON THE ORIGIN AND DESIGN OF GOVERNMENT IN GENERAL, WITH CONCISE REMARKS ON THE ENGLISH CONSTITUTION.

Some writers have so confounded society with government, as to leave little or no distinction between them; whereas they are not only different, but have different origins. Society is produced by our wants, and government by our wickedness; the former promotes our happiness *positively* by uniting our affections, the latter *negatively* by restraining our vices. The one encourages intercourse, the other creates distinctions. The first a patron, the last a punisher.

Society in every state is a blessing, but government even in its best state is but a necessary evil; in its worst state an intolerable one; for when we suffer, or are exposed to the same miseries *by a government*, which we might expect in a country *without government*, our calamity is heightened by reflecting that we furnish the means by which we suffer. Government, like dress, is the badge of lost innocence; the palaces of kings are built on the ruins of the bowers of paradise. For were the impulses of conscience clear, uniform, and irresistibly obeyed, man would need no other lawgiver; but that not being the case, he finds it necessary to surrender up a part of his property to furnish means for the protection of the rest; and this he is induced to do by the same prudence which in every other case advises him out of two evils to choose the least. *Wherefore*, security being the true design and end of government, it unanswerably follows that whatever *form* thereof appears most likely to ensure it to us, with the least expence and greatest benefit, is preferable to all others.

In order to gain a clear and just idea of the design and end of government, let us suppose a small number of persons settled in some sequestered part of the earth, unconnected with the rest, they will then represent the first peopling of any country, or of the world. In this state of natural liberty, society will be their first thought. A thousand motives will excite them thereto, the strength of one man is so unequal to his wants, and his mind so unfitted for perpetual solitude, that he is soon obliged to seek assistance and relief of another, who in his turn requires the same. Four or five united would be able to raise a tolerable dwelling in the midst of a wilderness, but *one* man might labour out of the common period of life without accomplishing any thing; when he had felled his timber he could not remove it, nor erect it after it was removed; hunger in the mean time would urge him from his work, and every different want call him a different way. Disease, nay even misfortune would be death, for though neither might be mortal, yet either would disable him from living, and reduce him to a state in which he might rather be said to perish than to die.

Thus necessity, like a gravitating power, would soon form our newly arrived emigrants into society, the reciprocal blessings of which, would supersede, and render the obligations of law and government unnecessary while they remained perfectly just to each other; but as nothing but heaven is impregnable to vice, it will unavoidably happen, that in proportion as they surmount the first difficulties of emigration, which bound them together in a common cause, they will begin to relax in their duty and attachment to each other; and this remissness, will point out the necessity, of establishing some form of government to supply the defect of moral virtue.

Some convenient tree will afford them a State-House, under the branches of which, the whole colony may assemble to deliberate on public matters. It is more than probable that their first laws will have the title only of Regulations, and be enforced by no other penalty than public disesteem. In this first parliament every man, by natural right, will have a seat.

But as the colony increases, the public concerns will increase likewise, and the distance at which the members may be separated, will render it too inconvenient for all of them to meet on every occasion as at first, when their number was small, their habitations near, and the public concerns few and trifling. This will point out the convenience of their consenting to leave the legislative part to be managed by a select number chosen from the whole body, who are supposed to have the same concerns at stake which those who appointed them, and who will act in the same manner as the whole body would act were they present. If the colony continue increasing, it will become necessary to augment the number of the representatives, and that the interest of every part of the colony may be attended to, it will be found best to divide the whole into convenient parts, each part sending its proper number; and that the *elected* might never form to themselves an interest separate from the *electors*, prudence will point out the propriety of having elections often; because as the *elected* might by that means return and mix again with the general body of the *electors* in a few months, their fidelity to the public will be secured by the prudent reflexion of not making a rod for themselves. And as this frequent interchange will establish a common interest with every part of the community, they will mutually and naturally support each other, and on this (not on the unmeaning name of king) depends the *strength of government, and the happiness of the governed.*

Here then is the origin and rise of government; namely, a mode rendered necessary by the inability of moral virtue to govern the world; here too is the design and end of government, viz. freedom and security. And however our eyes may be dazzled with show, or our ears deceived by sound; however prejudice may warp our wills, or interest darken our understanding, the simple voice of nature and of reason will say, it is right.

I draw my idea of the form of government from a principle in nature, which no art can overturn, viz. that the more simple any thing is, the less liable it is to be disordered; and the easier repaired when disordered; and with this maxim in view, I offer a few remarks on the so much boasted constitution of England. That it was noble for the dark and slavish times in which it was erected, is granted. When the world was over run with tyranny the least remove therefrom was a glorious rescue. But that it is imperfect, subject to convulsions, and incapable of producing what it seems to promise, is easily demonstrated.

Absolute governments (tho' the disgrace of human nature) have this advantage with them, that they are simple; if the people suffer, they know the head from which their suffering springs, know likewise the remedy, and are not bewildered by a variety of causes and cures. But the constitution of England is so exceedingly complex, that the nation may suffer for years together without being able to discover in which part the fault lies, some will say in one and some in another, and every political physician will advise a different medicine.

I know it is difficult to get over local or long standing prejudices, yet if we will suffer ourselves to examine the component parts of the English constitution, we shall find them to be the base remains of two ancient tyrannies, compounded with some new republican materials.

First.—The remains of monarchical tyranny in the person of the king.

Secondly.—The remains of aristocratical tyranny in the persons of the peers.

Thirdly.—The new republican materials, in the persons of the commons, on whose virtue depends the freedom of England.

The two first, by being hereditary, are independent of the people; wherefore in a *constitutional sense* they contribute nothing towards the freedom of the state.

To say that the constitution of England is a *union* of three powers reciprocally *checking* each other, is farcical, either the words have no meaning, or they are flat contradictions.

To say that the commons is a check upon the king, presupposes two things:

First.—That the king is not to be trusted without being looked after, or in other words, that a thirst for absolute power is the natural disease of monarchy.

Secondly.—That the commons, by being appointed for that purpose, are either wiser or more worthy of confidence than the crown.

But as the same constitution which gives the commons a power to check the king by withholding the supplies, gives afterwards the king a power to check the commons, by empowering him to reject their other bills; it again supposes that the king is wiser than those whom it has already supposed to be wiser than him. A mere absurdity!

There is something exceedingly ridiculous in the composition of monarchy; it first excludes a man from the means of information, yet empowers him to act in cases where the highest judgment is required. The state of a king shuts him from the world, yet the business of a king requires him to know it thoroughly; wherefore the different parts, by unnaturally opposing and destroying each other, prove the whole character to be absurd and useless.

Some writers have explained the English constitution thus; the king, say they, is one, the people another; the peers are an house in behalf of the king; the commons in behalf of the people; but this hath all the distinctions of a house divided against itself; and though the expressions be pleasantly arranged, yet when examined they appear idle and ambiguous; and it will always happen, that the nicest construction that words are capable of, when applied to the description of some thing which either cannot exist, or is too incomprehensible to be within the compass of description, will be words of sound only, and though they may amuse the ear, they cannot inform the mind, for this explanation includes a previous question, viz. *How came the king by a power which the people are afraid to trust, and always obliged to check?* Such a power could not be the gift of a wise people, neither can any power, *which needs checking*, be from God; yet the provision, which the constitution makes, supposes such a power to exist.

But the provision is unequal to the task; the means either cannot or will not accomplish the end, and the whole affair is a felo de se;

for as the greater weight will always carry up the less, and as all the wheels of a machine are put in motion by one, it only remains to know which power in the constitution has the most weight, for that will govern; and though the others, or a part of them, may clog, or, as the phrase is, check the rapidity of its motion, yet so long as they cannot stop it, their endeavors will be ineffectual; the first moving power will at last have its way, and what it wants in speed is supplied by time.

That the crown is this overbearing part in the English constitution needs not be mentioned, and that it derives its whole consequence merely from being the giver of places and pensions is self-evident, wherefore, though we have been wise enough to shut and lock a door against absolute monarchy, we at the same time have been foolish enough to put the crown in possession of the key.

The prejudice of Englishmen, in favour of their own government by king, lords and commons, arises as much or more from national pride than reason. Individuals are undoubtedly safer in England than in some other countries, but the *will* of the king is as much the *law* of the land in Britain as in France, with this difference, that instead of proceeding directly from his mouth, it is handed to the people under the more formidable shape of an act of parliament. For the fate of Charles the first, hath only made kings more subtle—not more just.

Wherefore, laying aside all national pride and prejudice in favour of modes and forms, the plain truth is, that *it is wholly owing to the constitution of the people, and not to the constitution of the government* that the crown is not as oppressive in England as in Turkey.

An inquiry into the *constitutional errors* in the English form of government is at this time highly necessary, for as we are never in a proper condition of doing justice to others, while we continue under the influence of some leading partiality, so neither are we capable of doing it to ourselves while we remain fettered by any obstinate prejudice. And as a man, who is attached to a prostitute, is unfitted to choose or judge of a wife, so any prepossession in favour of a rotten constitution of government will disable us from discerning a good one.

Of Monarchy and Hereditary Succession.

Mankind being originally equals in the order of creation, the equality could only be destroyed by some subsequent circumstance; the distinctions of rich, and poor, may in a great measure be accounted for, and that without having recourse to the harsh ill sounding names of oppression and avarice. Oppression is often the *consequence*, but seldom or never the *means* of riches; and though avarice will preserve a man from being necessitously poor, it generally makes him too timorous to be wealthy.

But there is another and greater distinction for which no truly natural or religious reason can be assigned, and that is, the distinction of men into kings and subjects. Male and female are the distinctions of nature, good and bad the distinctions of heaven; but how a race of men came into the world so exalted above the rest, and distinguished like some new species, is worth enquiring into, and whether they are the means of happiness or of misery to mankind.

In the early ages of the world, according to the scripture chronology, there were no kings; the consequence of which was there were no wars; it is the pride of kings which throw mankind into confusion. Holland without a king hath enjoyed more peace for this last century than any of the monarchial governments in Europe. Antiquity favors the same remark; for the quiet and rural lives of the first patriarchs hath a happy something in them, which vanishes away when we come to the history of Jewish royalty.

Government by kings was first introduced into the world by the Heathens, from whom the children of Israel copied the custom. It was the most prosperous invention the Devil ever set on foot for the promotion of idolatry. The Heathens paid divine honors to their deceased kings, and the christian world hath improved on the plan by doing the same to their living ones. How impious is the title of sacred majesty applied to a worm, who in the midst of his splendor is crumbling into dust!

As the exalting one man so greatly above the rest cannot be justified on the equal rights of nature, so neither can it be defended on the authority of scripture; for the will of the Almighty, as declared by Gideon and the prophet Samuel, expressly disapproves of government by kings. All anti-monarchical parts of scripture have been very smoothly glossed over in monarchical governments, but they undoubtedly merit the attention of countries which have their governments yet to form. "*Render unto Cæsar the things which are Cæsar's*" is the scripture doctrine of courts, yet it is no support of monarchical government, for the Jews at that time were without a king, and in a state of vassalage to the Romans.

Near three thousand years passed away from the Mosaic account of the creation, till the Jews under a national delusion requested a king. Till then their form of government (except in extraordinary cases, where the Almighty interposed) was a kind of republic administred by a judge and the elders of the tribes. Kings they had none, and it was held sinful to acknowledge any being under that title but the Lord of Hosts. And when a man seriously reflects on the idolatrous homage which is paid to the persons of Kings, he need not wonder, that the Almighty ever jealous of his honor, should disapprove of a form of government which so impiously invades the prerogative of heaven.

Monarchy is ranked in scripture as one of the sins of the Jews, for which a curse in reserve is denounced against them. The history of that transaction is worth attending to.

The children of Israel being oppressed by the Midianites, Gideon marched against them with a small army, and victory, thro' the divine interposition, decided in his favour. The Jews elate with success, and attributing it to the generalship of Gideon, proposed making him a king, saying, *Rule thou over us, thou and thy son and thy son's son.* Here was temptation in its fullest extent; not a kingdom only, but an hereditary one, but Gideon in the piety of his soul replied, *I will not rule over you, neither shall my son rule over you.* The Lord shall rule over you. Words need not be more explicit; Gideon doth not *decline* the honor, but denieth their right to give it; neither doth he compliment them with invented declarations of his thanks, but in the positive stile of a prophet charges them with disaffection to their proper Sovereign, the King of heaven.

About one hundred and thirty years after this, they fell again into the same error. The hankering which the Jews had for the idolatrous customs of the Heathens, is something exceedingly unaccountable; but so it was, that laying hold of the misconduct of Samuel's two sons, who were entrusted with some secular concerns, they came in an abrupt and clamorous manner to Samuel, saying, *Behold thou art old, and thy sons walk not in thy ways, now make us a king to judge us like all other nations.* And here we cannot but observe that their motives were bad, viz. that they might be *like* unto other nations, i.e. the Heathens, whereas their true glory laid in being as much *unlike* them as possible. *But the thing displeased Samuel when they said, Give us a king to judge us; and Samuel prayed unto the Lord, and the Lord said unto Samuel, Hearken unto the voice of the people in all that they say unto thee, for they have not rejected thee, but they have rejected me*, THAT I SHOULD NOT REIGN OVER THEM. *According to all the works which they have done since the day that I brought them up out of Egypt, even unto this day; wherewith they have forsaken me and served other Gods; so do they also unto thee. Now therefore hearken unto their voice, howbeit, protest solemnly unto them and shew them the manner of the king that shall reign over them, i.e.* not of any particular king, but the general manner of the kings of the earth, whom Israel was so eagerly copying after. And notwithstanding the great distance of time and difference of manners, the character is still in fashion. *And Samuel told all the words of the Lord unto the people, that asked of him a king. And he said, This shall be the manner of the king that shall reign over you; he will take your sons and appoint them for himself, for his chariots, and to be his horsemen, and some shall run before his chariots* (this description agrees with the present mode of impressing men) *and he will appoint him captains over thousands and captains over fifties, and will set them to ear his ground and to reap his harvest, and to make his instruments of war, and instruments of his chariots; and he will take your daughters to be confectionaries, and to be cooks and to be bakers* (this describes the expence and luxury as well as the oppression of kings) *and he will take your fields and your olive yards, even the best of them, and give them to his servants; and he will take the tenth of your feed, and of your vineyards, and give them to his officers and to his servants* (by which we see that bribery, corruption and favoritism are the standing vices of kings) *and he will take the tenth of your men servants, and your maid servants, and your goodliest young men and your asses, and put them to his work; and he will take the tenth of your sheep, and ye shall be his servants, and ye shall cry out in that day because of your king which ye shall have chosen,* and the Lord will not hear you in that day. This accounts for the continuation of monarchy; neither do the characters of the few good kings which have lived since, either sanctify the title, or blot out the sinfulness of the origin; the high encomium given of David takes no notice of him *officially as a king*, but only as a *man* after God's own heart. *Nevertheless the People refused to obey the voice of Samuel, and they said, Nay, but we will have a king over us, that we may be like all the nations, and that our king may judge us, and go out before us, and fight our battles.* Samuel continued to reason with them, but to no purpose; he set before them their ingratitude, but all would not avail; and seeing them fully bent on their folly, he cried out, *I will call unto the Lord, and he shall send thunder and rain* (which then was a punishment, being in the time of wheat harvest) *that ye may perceive and see that your wickedness is great which ye have done in the sight of the Lord,* in asking you a king. *So Samuel called unto the Lord, and the Lord sent thunder and rain that day, and all the people greatly feared the Lord and Samuel. And all the people said unto Samuel, Pray for thy servants unto the Lord thy God that we die not, for* we have added unto our sins this evil, to ask a king. These portions of scripture are direct and positive. They admit of no equivocal construction. That the Almighty hath here entered his protest against monarchical government is true, or the scripture is false. And a man hath good reason to believe that there is as much of king-craft, as priest-craft, in withholding the scripture from the public in Popish countries. For monarchy in every instance is the Popery of government.

To the evil of monarchy we have added that of hereditary succession; and as the first is a degradation and lessening of ourselves, so the second, claimed as a matter of right, is an insult and an imposition on posterity. For all men being originally equals, no *one* by *birth* could have a right to set up his own family in perpetual preference to all others for ever, and though himself might deserve *some* decent degree of honors of his cotemporaries, yet his descendants might be far too unworthy to inherit them. One of the strongest *natural* proofs of the folly of hereditary right in kings, is, that nature disapproves it, otherwise she would not so frequently turn it into ridicule by giving mankind an *ass for a lion*.

Secondly, as no man at first could possess any other public honors than were bestowed upon him, so the givers of those honors could have no power to give away the right of posterity, and though they might say "We choose you for *our* head," they could not, without manifest injustice to their children, say "that your children and your children's children shall reign over *ours* for ever." Because such an unwise, unjust, unnatural compact might (perhaps) in the next succession put them under the government of a rogue or a fool. Most wise men, in their private sentiments, have ever treated hereditary right with contempt; yet it is one of those evils, which when once established is not easily removed; many submit from fear, others from superstition, and the more powerful part shares with the king the plunder of the rest.

This is supposing the present race of kings in the world to have had an honorable origin; whereas it is more than probable, that could we take off the dark covering of antiquity, and trace them to their first rise, that we should find the first of them nothing better than the principal ruffian of some restless gang, whose savage manners or pre-eminence in subtility obtained him the title of chief among plunderers; and who by increasing in power, and extending his depredations, over-awed the quiet and defenceless to purchase their safety by frequent contributions. Yet his electors could have no idea of giving hereditary right to his descendants, because such a perpetual exclusion of themselves was incompatible with the free and unrestrained principles they professed to live by. Wherefore, hereditary succession in the early ages of monarchy could not take place as a matter of claim, but as something casual or complimental; but as few or no records were extant in those days, and traditional history stuffed with fables, it was very easy, after the lapse of a few generations, to trump up some superstitious tale, conveniently timed, Mahomet like, to cram hereditary right down the throats of the vulgar. Perhaps the disorders which threatened, or seemed to threaten, on the decease of a leader and the choice of a new one (for elections among ruffians could not be very orderly) induced many at first to favor hereditary pretensions; by which means it happened, as it hath happened since, that what at first was submitted to as a convenience, was afterwards claimed as a right.

England, since the conquest, hath known some few good monarchs, but groaned beneath a much larger number of bad ones; yet no man in his senses can say that their claim under William the Conqueror is a very honorable one. A French bastard landing with an armed banditti, and establishing himself king of England against the consent of the natives, is in plain terms a very paltry rascally original.—It certainly hath no divinity in it. However, it is needless to spend much time in exposing the folly of hereditary right; if there are any so weak as to believe it, let them promiscuously worship the ass and lion, and welcome. I shall neither copy their humility, nor disturb their devotion.

Yet I should be glad to ask how they suppose kings came at first? The question admits but of three answers, viz. either by lot, by election, or by usurpation. If the first king was taken by lot, it establishes a precedent for the next, which excludes hereditary succession. Saul was by lot, yet the succession was not hereditary, neither does it appear from that transaction there was any intention it ever should. If the first king of any country was by election, that likewise establishes a precedent for the next; for to say, that the *right* of all future generations is taken away, by the act of the first electors, in their choice not only of a king, but of a family of kings for ever, hath no parrallel in or out of scripture but the doctrine of original sin, which supposes the free will of all men lost in Adam; and from such comparison, and it will admit of no other, hereditary succession can derive no glory. For as in Adam all sinned, and as in the first electors all men obeyed; as in the one all mankind were subjected to Satan, and in the other to Sovereignty; as our innocence was lost in the first, and our authority in the last; and as both disable us from reassuming some former state and privilege, it unanswerably follows that original sin and hereditary succession are parellels. Dishonorable rank! Inglorious connexion! Yet the most subtile sophist cannot produce a juster simile.

As to usurpation, no man will be so hardy as to defend it; and that William the Conqueror was an usurper is a fact not to be contradicted. The plain truth is, that the antiquity of English monarchy will not bear looking into.

But it is not so much the absurdity as the evil of hereditary succession which concerns mankind. Did it ensure a race of good and wise men it would have the seal of divine authority, but as it opens a door to the *foolish*, the *wicked*, and the *improper*, it hath in it the nature of oppression. Men who look upon themselves born to reign, and others to obey, soon grow insolent; selected from the rest of mankind their minds are early poisoned by importance; and the world they act in differs so materially from the world at large, that they have but little opportunity of knowing its true interests, and when they succeed to the government are frequently the most ignorant and unfit of any throughout the dominions.

Another evil which attends hereditary succession is, that the throne is subject to be possessed by a minor at any age; all which time the regency, acting under the cover of a king, have every opportunity and inducement to betray their trust. The same national misfortune happens, when a king worn out with age and infirmity, enters the last stage of human weakness. In both these cases the public becomes a prey to every miscreant, who can tamper successfully with the follies either of age or infancy.

The most plausible plea, which hath ever been offered in favour of hereditary succession, is, that it preserves a nation from civil wars; and were this true, it would be weighty; whereas, it is the most barefaced falsity ever imposed upon mankind. The whole history of England disowns the fact. Thirty kings and two minors have reigned in that distracted kingdom since the conquest, in which time there have been (including the Revolution) no less than eight civil wars and nineteen rebellions. Wherefore instead of making for peace, it makes against it, and destroys the very foundation it seems to stand on.

The contest for monarchy and succession, between the houses of York and Lancaster, laid England in a scene of blood for many years.

Twelve pitched battles, besides skirmishes and sieges, were fought between Henry and Edward. Twice was Henry prisoner to Edward, who in his turn was prisoner to Henry. And so uncertain is the fate of war and the temper of a nation, when nothing but personal matters are the ground of a quarrel, that Henry was taken in triumph from a prison to a palace, and Edward obliged to fly from a palace to a foreign land; yet, as sudden transitions of temper are seldom lasting, Henry in his turn was driven from the throne, and Edward recalled to succeed him. The parliament always following the strongest side.

This contest began in the reign of Henry the Sixth, and was not entirely extinguished till Henry the Seventh, in whom the families were united. Including a period of 67 years, viz. from 1422 to 1489.

In short, monarchy and succession have laid (not this or that kingdom only) but the world in blood and ashes. 'Tis a form of government which the word of God bears testimony against, and blood will attend it.

If we inquire into the business of a king, we shall find that in some countries they have none; and after sauntering away their lives without pleasure to themselves or advantage to the nation, withdraw from the scene, and leave their successors to tread the same idle round. In absolute monarchies the whole weight of business, civil and military, lies on the king; the children of Israel in their request for a king, urged this plea "that he may judge us, and go out before us and fight our battles." But in countries where he is neither a judge nor a general, as in England, a man would be puzzled to know what *is* his business.

The nearer any government approaches to a republic the less business there is for a king. It is somewhat difficult to find a proper name for the government of England. Sir William Meredith calls it a republic; but in its present state it is unworthy of the name, because the corrupt influence of the crown, by having all the places in its disposal, hath so effectually swallowed up the power, and eaten out the virtue of the house of commons (the republican part in the constitution) that the government of England is nearly as monarchical as that of France or Spain. Men fall out with names without understanding them. For it is the republican and not the monarchical part of the constitution of England which Englishmen glory in, viz. the liberty of choosing a house of commons from out of their own body—and it is easy to see that when republican virtue fails, slavery ensues. Why is the constitution of England sickly, but because monarchy hath poisoned the republic, the crown hath engrossed the commons?

In England a king hath little more to do than to make war and give away places; which in plain terms, is to impoverish the nation and set it together by the ears. A pretty business indeed for a man to be allowed eight hundred thousand sterling a year for, and worshipped into the bargain! Of more worth is one honest man to society and in the sight of God, than all the crowned ruffians that ever lived.

Thoughts on the Present State of American Affairs.

In the following pages I offer nothing more than simple facts, plain arguments, and common sense; and have no other preliminaries to settle with the reader, than that he will divest himself of prejudice and prepossession, and suffer his reason and his feelings to determine for themselves; that he will put *on*, or rather that he will not put *off*, the true character of a man, and generously enlarge his views beyond the present day.

Volumes have been written on the subject of the struggle between England and America. Men of all ranks have embarked in the controversy, from different motives, and with various designs; but all have been ineffectual, and the period of debate is closed. Arms, as the last resource, decide the contest; the appeal was the choice of the king, and the continent hath accepted the challenge.

It hath been reported of the late Mr. Pelham (who tho' an able minister was not without his faults) that on his being attacked in the house of commons, on the score, that his measures were only of a temporary kind, replied "*they will last my time.*" Should a thought so fatal and unmanly possess the colonies in the present contest, the name of ancestors will be remembered by future generations with detestation.

The sun never shined on a cause of greater worth. 'Tis not the affair of a city, a country, a province, or a kingdom, but of a continent—of at least one eighth part of the habitable globe. 'Tis not the concern of a day, a year, or an age; posterity are virtually involved in the contest, and will be more or less affected, even to the end of time, by the proceedings now. Now is the seed time of continental union, faith and honor. The least fracture now will be like a name engraved with the point of a pin on the tender rind of a young oak; the wound will enlarge with the tree, and posterity read it in full grown characters.

By referring the matter from argument to arms, a new æra for politics is struck; a new method of thinking hath arisen. All plans, proposals, &c. prior to the nineteenth of April, *i.e.* to the commencement of hostilities, are like the almanacks of the last year; which, though proper then, are superseded and useless now. Whatever was advanced by the advocates on either side of the question then, terminated in one and the same point, viz. a union with Great-Britain; the only difference between the parties was the method of effecting it; the one proposing force, the other friendship; but it hath so far happened that the first hath failed, and the second hath withdrawn her influence.

As much hath been said of the advantages of reconciliation, which, like an agreeable dream, hath passed away and left us as we were, it is but right, that we should examine the contrary side of the argument, and inquire into some of the many material injuries which these colonies sustain, and always will sustain, by being connected with, and dependant on Great-Britain. To examine that connexion and dependance, on the principles of nature and common sense, to see what we have to trust to, if separated, and what we are to expect, if dependant.

I have heard it asserted by some, that as America hath flourished under her former connexion with Great-Britain, that the same connexion is necessary towards her future happiness, and will always have the same effect. Nothing can be more fallacious than this kind of argument. We may as well assert that because a child has thrived upon milk, that it is never to have meat, or that the first twenty years of our lives is to become a precedent for the next twenty. But even this is admitting more than is true, for I answer roundly, that America would have flourished as much, and probably much more, had no European power had any thing to do with her. The commerce, by which she hath enriched herself are the necessaries of life, and will always have a market while eating is the custom of Europe.

But she has protected us, say some. That she has engrossed us is true, and defended the continent at our expence as well as her own is admitted, and she would have defended Turkey from the same motive, viz. the sake of trade and dominion.

Alas, we have been long led away by ancient prejudices, and made large sacrifices to superstition. We have boasted the protection of Great-Britain, without considering, that her motive was *interest* not *attachment*; that she did not protect us from *our enemies* on *our account*, but from *her enemies* on *her own account*, from those who had no quarrel with us on any *other account*, and who will always be our enemies on the *same account*. Let Britain wave her pretensions to the continent, or the continent throw off the dependance, and we should be at peace with France and Spain were they at war with Britain. The miseries of Hanover last war ought to warn us against connexions.

It has lately been asserted in parliament, that the colonies have no relation to each other but through the parent country, *i.e.* that Pennsylvania and the Jerseys, and so on for the rest, are sister colonies by the way of England; this is certainly a very round-about way of proving relationship, but it is the nearest and only true way of proving enemyship, if I may so call it. France and Spain never were, nor perhaps ever will be our enemies as *Americans*, but as our being the *subjects of Great-Britain*.

But Britain is the parent country, say some. Then the more shame upon her conduct. Even brutes do not devour their young, nor savages make war upon their families; wherefore the assertion, if true, turns to her reproach; but it happens not to be true, or only partly so, and the phrase *parent* or *mother country* hath been jesuitically adopted by the king and his parasites, with a low papistical design of gaining an unfair bias on the credulous weakness of our minds. Europe, and not England, is the parent country of America. This new world hath been the asylum for the persecuted lovers of civil and religious liberty from *every part* of Europe. Hither have they fled, not from the tender embraces of the mother, but from the cruelty of the monster; and it is so far true of England, that the same tyranny which drove the first emigrants from home, pursues their descendants still.

In this extensive quarter of the globe, we forget the narrow limits of three hundred and sixty miles (the extent of England) and carry our friendship on a larger scale; we claim brotherhood with every European christian, and triumph in the generosity of the sentiment.

It is pleasant to observe by what regular gradations we surmount the force of local prejudice, as we enlarge our acquaintance with the world. A man born in any town in England divided into parishes, will naturally associate most with his fellow parishioners (because their interests in many cases will be common) and distinguish him by the name of *neighbour*; if he meet him but a few miles from home, he drops the narrow idea of a street, and salutes him by the name of *townsman*; if he travel out of the county, and meet him in any other, he forgets the minor divisions of street and town, and calls him *countryman*, i.e. *county-man*; but if in their foreign excursions they should associate in France or any other part of *Europe*, their local remembrance would be enlarged into that of *Englishmen*. And by a just parity of reasoning, all Europeans meeting in America, or any other quarter of the globe, are *countrymen*; for England, Holland, Germany, or Sweden, when compared with the whole, stand in the same places on the larger scale, which the divisions of street, town, and county do on the smaller ones; distinctions too limited for continental minds. Not one third of the inhabitants, even of this province, are of English descent. Wherefore I reprobate the phrase of parent or mother country applied to England only, as being false, selfish, narrow and ungenerous.

But admitting, that we were all of English descent, what does it amount to? Nothing. Britain, being now an open enemy, extinguishes every other name and title: And to say that reconciliation is our duty, is truly farcical. The first king of England, of the present line (William the Conqueror) was a Frenchman, and half the Peers of England are descendants from the same country; therefore, by the same method of reasoning, England ought to be governed by France.

Much hath been said of the united strength of Britain and the colonies, that in conjunction they might bid defiance to the world. But this is mere presumption; the fate of war is uncertain, neither do the expressions mean any thing; for this continent would never suffer itself to be drained of inhabitants, to support the British arms in either Asia, Africa, or Europe.

Besides what have we to do with setting the world at defiance? Our plan is commerce, and that, well attended to, will secure us the peace and friendship of all Europe; because, it is the interest of all Europe to have America a *free port.* Her trade will always be a protection, and her barrenness of gold and silver secure her from invaders.

I challenge the warmest advocate for reconciliation, to shew, a single advantage that this continent can reap, by being connected with Great Britain. I repeat the challenge, not a single advantage is derived. Our corn will fetch its price in any market in Europe, and our imported goods must be paid for buy them where we will.

But the injuries and disadvantages we sustain by that connection, are without number; and our duty to mankind at large, as well as to ourselves, instruct us to renounce the alliance: Because, any submission to, or dependance on Great-Britain, tends directly to involve this continent in European wars and quarrels; and sets us at variance with nations, who would otherwise seek our friendship, and against whom, we have neither anger nor complaint. As Europe is our market for trade, we ought to form no partial connection with any part of it. It is the true interest of America to steer clear of European contentions, which she never can do, while by her dependence on Britain, she is made the make-weight in the scale of British politics.

Europe is too thickly planted with kingdoms to be long at peace, and whenever a war breaks out between England and any foreign power, the trade of America goes to ruin, *because of her connection with Britain.* The next war may not turn out like the last, and should it not, the advocates for reconciliation now will be wishing for separation then, because, neutrality in that case, would be a safer convoy than a man of war. Every thing that is right or natural pleads for separation. The blood of the slain, the weeping voice of nature cries, 'Tis time to part. Even the distance at which the Almighty hath placed

England and America, is a strong and natural proof, that the authority of the one, over the other, was never the design of Heaven. The time likewise at which the continent was discovered, adds weight to the argument, and the manner in which it was peopled encreases the force of it. The reformation was preceded by the discovery of America, as if the Almighty graciously meant to open a sanctuary to the persecuted in future years, when home should afford neither friendship nor safety.

The authority of Great-Britain over this continent, is a form of government, which sooner or later must have an end: And a serious mind can draw no true pleasure by looking forward, under the painful and positive conviction, that what he calls "the present constitution" is merely temporary. As parents, we can have no joy, knowing that *this government* is not sufficiently lasting to ensure any thing which we may bequeath to posterity: And by a plain method of argument, as we are running the next generation into debt, we ought to do the work of it, otherwise we use them meanly and pitifully. In order to discover the line of our duty rightly, we should take our children in our hand, and fix our station a few years farther into life; that eminence will present a prospect, which a few present fears and prejudices conceal from our sight.

Though I would carefully avoid giving unnecessary offence, yet I am inclined to believe, that all those who espouse the doctrine of reconciliation, may be included within the following descriptions. Interested men, who are not to be trusted; weak men, who *cannot* see; prejudiced men, who *will not* see; and a certain set of moderate men, who think better of the European world than it deserves; and this last class, by an ill-judged deliberation, will be the cause of more calamities to this continent, than all the other three.

It is the good fortune of many to live distant from the scene of sorrow; the evil is not sufficient brought to *their* doors to make *them* feel the precariousness with which all American property is possessed. But let our imaginations transport us for a few moments to Boston, that seat of wretchedness will teach us wisdom, and instruct us for ever to renounce a power in whom we can have no trust. The inhabitants of that unfortunate city, who but a few months ago were in ease and affluence, have now, no other alternative than to stay and starve, or turn out to beg. Endangered by the fire of their friends if they continue within the city, and plundered by the soldiery if they leave it. In their present condition they are prisoners without the hope of redemption, and in a general attack for their relief, they would be exposed to the fury of both armies.

Men of passive tempers look somewhat lightly over the offences of Britain, and, still hoping for the best, are apt to call out, "*Come, come, we shall be friends again, for all this.*" But examine the passions and feelings of mankind, Bring the doctrine of reconciliation to the touchstone of nature, and then tell me, whether you can hereafter love, honour, and faithfully serve the power that hath carried fire and sword into your land? If you cannot do all these, then are you only deceiving yourselves, and by your delay bringing ruin upon posterity. Your future connection with Britain, whom you can neither love nor honour, will be forced and unnatural, and being formed only on the plan of present convenience, will in a little time fall into a relapse more wretched than the first. But if you say, you can still pass the violations over, then I ask, Hath your house been burnt? Hath your property been destroyed before your face? Are your wife and children destitute of a bed to lie on, or bread to live on? Have you lost a parent or a child by their hands, and yourself the ruined and wretched survivor? If you have not, then are you not a judge of those who have. But if you have, and still can shake hands with the murderers, then are you unworthy of the name of husband, father, friend, or lover, and whatever may be your rank or title in life, you have the heart of a coward, and the spirit of a sycophant.

This is not inflaming or exaggerating matters, but trying them by those feelings and affections which nature justifies, and without which, we should be incapable of discharging the social duties of life, or enjoying the felicities of it. I mean not to exhibit horror for the purpose of provoking revenge, but to awaken us from fatal and unmanly slumbers, that we may pursue determinately some fixed object. It is not in the power of Britain or of Europe to conquer America, if she do not conquer herself by *delay* and *timidity*. The present winter is worth an age if rightly employed, but if lost or neglected, the whole continent will partake of the misfortune; and there is no punishment which that man will not deserve, be he who, or what, or where he will, that may be the means of sacrificing a season so precious and useful.

It is repugnant to reason, to the universal order of things to all examples from former ages, to suppose, that this continent can longer remain subject to any external power. The most sanguine in Britain does not think so. The utmost stretch of human wisdom cannot, at this time, compass a plan short of separation, which can promise the continent even a year's security. Reconciliation is *now* a fallacious dream. Nature hath deserted the connexion, and Art cannot supply her place. For, as Milton wisely expresses, "never can true reconcilement grow where wounds of deadly hate have pierced so deep."

Every quiet method for peace hath been ineffectual. Our prayers have been rejected with disdain; and only tended to convince us, that nothing flatters vanity, or confirms obstinacy in Kings more than repeated petitioning—and nothing hath contributed more than that very measure to make the Kings of Europe absolute: Witness Denmark and Sweden. Wherefore, since nothing but blows will do, for God's sake, let us come to a final separation, and not leave the next generation to be cutting throats, under the violated unmeaning names of parent and child.

To say, they will never attempt it again is idle and visionary, we thought so at the repeal of the stamp-act, yet a year or two undeceived us; as well may we suppose that nations, which have been once defeated, will never renew the quarrel.

As to government matters, it is not in the power of Britain to do this continent justice: The business of it will soon be too weighty, and intricate, to be managed with any tolerable degree of convenience, by a power, so distant from us, and so very ignorant of us; for if they cannot conquer us, they cannot govern us. To be always running three or four thousand miles with a tale or a petition, waiting four or five months for an answer, which when obtained requires five or six more to explain it in, will in a few years be looked upon as folly and childishness—There was a time when it was proper, and there is a proper time for it to cease.

Small islands not capable of protecting themselves, are the proper objects for kingdoms to take under their care; but there is something very absurd, in supposing a continent to be perpetually governed by an island. In no instance hath nature made the satellite larger than its primary planet, and as England and America, with respect to each other, reverses the common order of nature, it is evident they belong to different systems: England to Europe, America to itself.

I am not induced by motives of pride, party, or resentment to espouse the doctrine of separation and independance; I am clearly, positively, and conscientiously persuaded that it is the true interest of this continent to be so; that every thing short of *that* is mere patchwork, that it can afford no lasting felicity,—that it is leaving the sword to our children, and shrinking back at a time, when, a little more, a little farther, would have rendered this continent the glory of the earth.

As Britain hath not manifested the least inclination towards a compromise, we may be assured that no terms can be obtained worthy the acceptance of the continent, or any ways equal to the expence of blood and treasure we have been already put to.

The object, contended for, ought always to bear some just proportion to the expence. The removal of North, or the whole detestable junto, is a matter unworthy the millions we have expended. A temporary stoppage of trade, was an inconvenience, which would have sufficiently ballanced the repeal of all the acts complained of, had such repeals been obtained; but if the whole continent must take up arms, if every man must be a soldier, it is scarcely worth our while to fight against a contemptible ministry only. Dearly, dearly, do we pay for the repeal of the acts, if that is all we fight for; for in a just estimation, it is as great a folly to pay a Bunker-hill price for law, as for land. As I have always considered the independancy of this continent, as an event, which sooner or later must arrive, so from the late rapid progress of the continent to maturity, the event could not be far off. Wherefore, on the breaking out of hostilities, it was not worth the while to have disputed a matter, which time would have finally redressed, unless we meant to be in earnest; otherwise, it is like wasting an estate on a suit at law, to regulate the trespasses of a tenant, whose lease is just expiring. No man was a warmer wisher for reconciliation than myself, before the fatal nineteenth of April 1775, but the moment the event of that day was made known, I rejected the hardened, sullen tempered Pharaoh of England for ever; and disdain the wretch, that with the pretended title of father of his people can unfeelingly hear of their slaughter, and composedly sleep with their blood upon his soul.

But admitting that matters were now made up, what would be the event? I answer, the ruin of the continent. And that for several reasons.

First. The powers of governing still remaining in the hands of the king, he will have a negative over the whole legislation of this continent. And as he hath shewn himself such an inveterate enemy to liberty, and discovered such a thirst for arbitrary power; is he, or is he not, a proper man to say to these colonies, "*You shall make no laws but what I please*." And is there any inhabitant in America so ignorant, as not to know, that according to what is called the *present constitution*, that this continent can make no laws but what the king gives leave to; and is there any man so unwise, as not to see, that (considering what has happened) he will suffer no law to be made here, but such as suit *his* purpose. We may be as effectually enslaved by the want of laws in America, as by submitting to laws made for us in England. After matters are made up (as it is called) can there be any doubt, but the whole power of the crown will be exerted, to keep this continent as low and humble as possible? Instead of going forward we shall go backward, or be perpetually quarrelling or ridiculously petitioning.—We are already greater than the king wishes us to be, and will he not hereafter endeavour to make us less? To bring the matter to one point. Is the power who is jealous of our prosperity, a proper power to govern us? Whoever says *No* to this question is an *independant*, for independancy means no more, than, whether we shall make our own laws, or whether the king, the greatest enemy this continent hath, or can have, shall tell us "*there shall be no laws but such as I like*."

But the king you will say has a negative in England; the people there can make no laws without his consent. In point of right and good order, there is something very ridiculous, that a youth of twenty-one (which hath often happened) shall say to several millions of people, older and wiser than himself, I forbid this or that act of yours to be law. But in this place I decline this sort of reply, though I will never cease to expose the absurdity of it, and only answer, that England being the King's residence, and America not so, makes quite another case. The king's negative *here* is ten times more dangerous and fatal than it can be in England, for *there* he will scarcely refuse his consent to a bill for putting England into as strong a state of defence as possible, and in America he would never suffer such a bill to be passed.

America is only a secondary object in the system of British politics, England consults the good of *this* country, no farther than it answers her *own* purpose. Wherefore, her own interest leads her to suppress the growth of *ours* in every case which doth not promote her advantage, or in the least interferes with it. A pretty state we should soon be in under such a second-hand government, considering what has happened! Men do not change from enemies to friends by the alteration of a name: And in order to shew that reconciliation *now* is a dangerous doctrine, I affirm, *that it would be policy in the king at this time, to repeal the acts for the sake of reinstating himself in the government of the provinces;* in order, that he may accomplish by craft and subtilty, in the long run, what he cannot do by force and violence in the short one. Reconciliation and ruin are nearly related.

Secondly. That as even the best terms, which we can expect to obtain, can amount to no more than a temporary expedient, or a kind of government by guardianship, which can last no longer than till the colonies come of age, so the general face and state of things, in the interim, will be unsettled and unpromising. Emigrants of property will not choose to come to a country whose form of government hangs but by a thread, and who is every day tottering on the brink of commotion and disturbance; and numbers of the present inhabitants would lay hold of the interval, to dispense of their effects, and quit the continent.

But the most powerful of all arguments, is, that nothing but independance, i.e. a continental form of government, can keep the peace of the continent and preserve it inviolate from civil wars. I dread the event of a reconciliation with Britain now, as it is more than probable, that it will be followed by a revolt somewhere or other, the consequences of which may be far more fatal than all the malice of Britain.

Thousands are already ruined by British barbarity. Thousands more will probably suffer the same fate. Those men have other feelings than us who have nothing suffered. All they *now* possess is liberty, what they before enjoyed is sacrificed to its service, and having nothing more to lose, they disdain submission. Besides, the general temper of the colonies, towards a British government, will be like that of a youth, who is nearly out of his time; they will care very little about her. And a government which cannot preserve the peace, is no government at all, and in that case we pay our money for nothing; and pray what is it that Britain can do, whose power will be wholly on paper, should a civil tumult break out the very day after reconciliation? I have heard some men say, many of whom I believe spoke without thinking, that they dreaded an independance, fearing that it would produce civil wars. It is but seldom that our first thoughts are truly correct, and that is the case here; for there are ten times more to dread from a patched up connexion than from independance. I make the sufferers case my own, and I protest, that were I driven from house and home, my property destroyed, and my circumstances ruined, that as man, sensible of injuries, I could never relish the doctrine of reconciliation, or consider myself bound thereby.

The colonies have manifested such a spirit of good order and obedience to continental government, as is sufficient to make every reasonable person easy and happy on that head. No man can assign the least pretence for his fears, on any other grounds, than such as are truly childish and ridiculous, viz. that one colony will be striving for superiority over another.

Where there are no distinctions there can be no superiority, perfect equality affords no temptation. The republics of Europe are all (and we may say always) in peace. Holland and Swisserland are without wars, foreign or domestic: Monarchical governments, it is true, are never long at rest; the crown itself is a temptation to enterprizing ruffians at *home*; and that degree of pride and insolence ever attendant on regal authority, swells into a rupture with foreign powers, in instances, where a republican government, by being formed on more natural principles, would negotiate the mistake.

If there is any true cause of fear respecting independance, it is because no plan is yet laid down. Men do not see their way out—Wherefore, as an opening into that business, I offer the following hints; at the same time modestly affirming, that I have no other opinion of them myself, than that they may be the means of giving rise to something better. Could the straggling thoughts of individuals be collected, they would frequently form materials for wise and able men to improve into useful matter.

Let the assemblies be annual, with a President only. The representation more equal. Their business wholly domestic, and subject to the authority of a Continental Congress.

Let each colony be divided into six, eight, or ten, convenient districts, each district to send a proper number of delegates to Congress, so that each colony send at least thirty. The whole number in Congress will be at least 390. Each Congress to sit and to choose a president by the following method. When the delegates are met, let a colony be taken from the whole thirteen colonies by lot, after which, let the whole Congress choose (by ballot) a president from out of the delegates of *that* province. In the next Congress, let a colony be taken by lot from twelve only, omitting that colony from which the president was taken in the former Congress, and so proceeding on till the whole thirteen shall have had their proper rotation. And in order that nothing may pass into a law but what is satisfactorily just, not less than three fifths of the Congress to be called a majority.—He that will promote discord, under a government so equally formed as this, would have joined Lucifer in his revolt.

But as there is a peculiar delicacy, from whom, or in what manner, this business must first arise, and as it seems most agreeable and consistent that it should come from some intermediate body between the governed and the governors, that is, between the Congress and the people, let a Continental Conference be held, in the following manner, and for the following purpose.

A committee of twenty-six members of Congress, viz. two for each colony. Two members from each House of Assembly, or Provincial Convention; and five representatives of the people at large, to be chosen in the capital city or town of each province, for, and in behalf of the whole province, by as many qualified voters as shall think proper to attend from all parts of the province for that purpose; or, if more convenient, the representatives may be chosen in two or three of the most populous parts thereof. In this conference, thus assembled, will be united, the two grand principles of business, *knowledge* and *power*. The members of Congress, Assemblies, or Conventions, by having had experience in national concerns, will be able and useful counsellors, and the whole, being impowered by the people, will have a truly legal authority.

The conferring members being met, let their business be to frame a Continental Charter, or Charter of the United Colonies; (answering to what is called the Magna Charta of England) fixing the number and manner of choosing members of Congress, members of Assembly, with their date of sitting, and drawing the line of business and jurisdiction between them: (Always remembering, that our strength is continental, not provincial:) Securing freedom and property to all men, and above all things, the free exercise of religion, according to the dictates of conscience; with such other matter as is necessary for a charter to contain. Immediately after which, the said Conference to dissolve, and the bodies which shall be chosen comformable to the said charter, to be the legislators and governors of this continent for the time being: Whose peace and happiness, may God preserve, Amen.

Should any body of men be hereafter delegated for this or some similar purpose, I offer them the following extracts from that wise observer on governments *Dragonetti*. "The science" says he "of the politician consists in fixing the true point of happiness and freedom. Those men would deserve the gratitude of ages, who should discover a mode of government that contained the greatest sum of individual happiness, with the least national expense. (Dragonetti on "Virtue and Rewards.")

But where says some is the King of America? I'll tell you Friend, he reigns above, and doth not make havoc of mankind like the Royal

Brute of Britain. Yet that we may not appear to be defective even in earthly honors, let a day be solemnly set apart for proclaiming the charter; let it be brought forth placed on the divine law, the word of God; let a crown be placed thereon, by which the world may know, that so far as we approve of monarchy, that in America the law is king. For as in absolute governments the King is law, so in free countries the law *ought* to be King; and there ought to be no other. But lest any ill use should afterwards arise, let the crown at the conclusion of the ceremony be demolished, and scattered among the people whose right it is.

A government of our own is our natural right: And when a man seriously reflects on the precariousness of human affairs, he will become convinced, that it is infinitely wiser and safer, to form a constitution of our own in a cool deliberate manner, while we have it in our power, than to trust such an interesting event to time and chance. If we omit it now, some Massanello* may hereafter arise, who laying hold of popular disquietudes, may collect together the desperate and the discontented, and by assuming to themselves the powers of government, may sweep away the liberties of the continent like a deluge. Should the government of America return again into the hands of Britain, the tottering situation of things, will be a temptation for some desperate adventurer to try his fortune; and in such a case, what relief can Britain give? Ere she could hear the news, the fatal business might be done; and ourselves suffering like the wretched Britons under the oppression of the Conqueror. Ye that oppose independance now, ye know not what ye do; ye are opening a door to eternal tyranny, by keeping vacant the seat of government. There are thousands, and tens of thousands, who would think it glorious to expel from the continent, that barbarous and hellish power, which hath stirred up the Indians and Negroes to destroy us, the cruelty hath a double guilt, it is dealing brutally by us, and treacherously by them.

*Thomas Anello, otherwise Massanello, a fisherman of Naples, who after spiriting up his countrymen in the public market place, against the oppressions of the Spaniards, to whom the place was then subject, prompted them to revolt, and in the space of a day became king.

To talk of friendship with those in whom our reason forbids us to have faith, and our affections wounded through a thousand pores instruct us to detest, is madness and folly. Every day wears out the little remains of kindred between us and them, and can there be any reason to hope, that as the relationship expires, the affection will increase, or that we shall agree better, when we have ten times more and greater concerns to quarrel over than ever?

Ye that tell us of harmony and reconciliation, can ye restore to us the time that is past? Can ye give to prostitution its former innocence? Neither can ye reconcile Britain and America. The last cord now is broken, the people of England are presenting addresses against us. There are injuries which nature cannot forgive; she would cease to be nature if she did. As well can the lover forgive the ravisher of his mistress, as the continent forgive the murders of Britain. The Almighty hath implanted in us these unextinguishable feelings for good and wise purposes. They are the guardians of his image in our hearts. They distinguish us from the herd of common animals. The social compact would dissolve, and justice be extirpated from the earth, or have only a casual existence were we callous to the touches of affection. The robber, and the murderer, would often escape unpunished, did not the injuries which our tempers sustain, provoke us into justice.

O ye that love mankind! Ye that dare oppose, not only the tyranny, but the tyrant, stand forth! Every spot of the old world is overrun with oppression. Freedom hath been hunted round the globe. Asia, and Africa, have long expelled her—Europe regards her like a stranger, and England hath given her warning to depart. O! receive the fugitive, and prepare in time an asylum for mankind.

Appendix B

Thoughts on Government

John Adams

1776

My dear Sir,

If I was equal to the task of forming a plan for the government of a colony, I should be flattered with your request, and very happy to comply with it; because, as the divine science of politics is the science of social happiness, and the blessings of society depend entirely on the constitutions of government, which are generally institutions that last for many generations, there can be no employment more agreeable to a benevolent mind than a research after the best.

Pope flattered tyrants too much when he said,

"For forms of government let fools contest, That which is best administered is best."

Nothing can be more fallacious than this. But poets read history to collect flowers, not fruits; they attend to fanciful images, not the effects of social institutions. Nothing is more certain, from the history of nations and nature of man, than that some forms of government are better fitted for being well administered than others.

We ought to consider what is the end of government, before we determine which is the best form. Upon this point all speculative politicians will agree, that the happiness of society is the end of government, as all divines and moral philosophers will agree that the happiness of the individual is the end of man. From this principle it will follow, that the form of government which communicates ease, comfort, security, or, in one word, happiness, to the greatest number of persons, and in the greatest degree, is the best.

All sober inquirers after truth, ancient and modern, pagan and Christian, have declared that the happiness of man, as well as his dignity, consists in virtue. Confucius, Zoroaster, Socrates, Mahomet, not to mention authorities really sacred, have agreed in this.

If there is a form of government, then, whose principle and foundation is virtue, will not every sober man acknowledge it better calculated to promote the general happiness than any other form?

Fear is the foundation of most governments; but it is so sordid and brutal a passion, and renders men in whose breasts it predominates so stupid and miserable, that Americans will not be likely to approve of any political institution which is founded on it.

Honor is truly sacred, but holds a lower rank in the scale of moral excellence than virtue. Indeed, the former is but a part of the latter, and consequently has not equal pretensions to support a frame of government productive of human happiness. The foundation of every government is some principle or passion in the minds of the people. The noblest principles and most generous affections in our nature, then, have the fairest chance to support the noblest and most generous models of government.

A man must be indifferent to the sneers of modern Englishmen, to mention in their company the names of Sidney, Harrington, Locke, Milton, Nedham, Neville, Burnet, and Hoadly. No small fortitude is necessary to confess that one has read them. The wretched condition of this country, however, for ten or fifteen years past, has frequently reminded me of their principles and reasonings. They will convince any candid mind, that there is no good government but what is republican. That the only valuable part of the British constitution is so; because the very definition of a republic is "an empire of laws, and not of men." That, as a republic is the best of governments, so that particular arrangement of the powers of society, or, in other words, that form of government which is best contrived to secure an impartial and exact execution of the laws, is the best of republics.

Of republics there is an inexhaustible variety, because the possible combinations of the powers of society are capable of innumerable variations.

As good government is an empire of laws, how shall your laws be made? In a large society, inhabiting an extensive country, it is impossible that the whole should assemble to make laws. The first necessary step, then, is to depute power from the many to a few of the most wise and good. But by what rules shall you choose your representatives? Agree upon the number and qualifications of persons who shall have the benefit of choosing, or annex this privilege to the inhabitants of a certain extent of ground.

The principle difficulty lies, and the greatest care should be employed in constituting this representative assembly. It should be in miniature an exact portrait of the people at large. It should think, feel, reason and act like them. That it may be the interest of this assembly to do strict justice at all times, it should be an equal representation, or, in other words, equal interests among the people should have equal interests in it. Great care should be taken to effect this, and to prevent unfair, partial, and corrupt elections. Such regulations, however, may be better made in times of greater tranquility than the present; and they will spring up themselves naturally, when all the powers of government come to be in the hands of the people's friends. At present, it will be safest to proceed in all established modes, to which the people have been familiarized by habit.

A representation of the people in one assembly being obtained, a question arises, whether all the powers of government, legislative, executive, and judicial, shall be left in this body? I think a people cannot be long free, nor ever happy, whose government is in one assembly. My reasons for this opinion are as follow:—

1. A single assembly is liable to all the vices, follies, and frailties of an individual; subject to fits of humor, starts of passion, flights of enthusiasm, partialities, or prejudice, and consequently productive of hasty results and absurd judgments. And all these errors ought to be corrected and defects supplied by some controlling power.

2. A single assembly is apt to be avaricious, and in time will not scruple to exempt itself from burdens, which it will lay, without compunction, on its constituents.

3. A single assembly is apt to grow ambitious, and after a time will not hesitate to vote itself perpetual. This was one fault of the Long Parliament; but more remarkably of Holland, whose assembly first voted themselves from annual to septennial, then for life, and after a course of years, that all vacancies happening by death or otherwise, should be filled by themselves, without any application to constituents at all.

4. A representative assembly, although extremely well qualified, and absolutely necessary, as a branch of the legislative, is unfit to exercise the executive power, for want of two essential properties, secrecy and dispatch.

5. A representative assembly is still less qualified for the judicial power, because it is too numerous, too slow, and too little skilled in the laws.

6. Because a single assembly, possessed of all the powers of government, would make arbitrary laws for their own interest, execute all laws arbitrarily for their own interest, and adjudge all controversies in their own favor.

But shall the whole power of legislation rest in one assembly? Most of the foregoing reasons apply equally to prove that the legislative power ought to be more complex; to which we may add, that if the legislative power is wholly in one assembly, and the executive in another, or in a single person, these two powers will oppose and encroach upon each other, until the contest shall end in war, and the whole power, legislative and executive, be usurped by the strongest.

The judicial power, in such case, could not mediate, or hold the balance between the two contending powers, because the legislative would undermine it. And this shows the necessity, too, of giving the executive power a negative upon the legislative, otherwise this will be continually encroaching upon that.

To avoid these dangers, let a distinct assembly be constituted, as a mediator between the two extreme branches of the legislature, that which represents the people, and that which is vested with the executive power.

Let the representative assembly then elect by ballot, from among themselves or their constituents, or both, a distinct assembly, which, for the sake of perspicuity, we will call a council. It may consist of any number you please, say twenty or thirty, and should have a free and independent exercise of its judgment, and consequently a negative voice in the legislature.

These two bodies, thus constituted, and made integral parts of the legislature, let them unite, and by joint ballot choose a governor, who, after being stripped of most of those badges of domination, called prerogatives, should have a free and independent exercise of his judgment, and be made also an integral part of the legislature. This, I know, is liable to objections; and, if you please, you may make him only president of the council, as in Connecticut. But as the governor is to be invested with the executive power, with consent of council, I think he ought to have a negative upon the legislative. If he is annually elective, as he ought to be, he will always have so much reverence and affection for the people, their representatives and counselors, that, although you give him an independent exercise of his judgment, he will seldom use it in opposition to the two houses, except in cases the public utility of which would be conspicuous; and some such cases would happen.

In the present exigency of American affairs, when, by an act of Parliament, we are put out of the royal protection, and consequently discharged from our allegiance, and it has become necessary to assume government for our immediate security, the governor, lieutenant-governor, secretary, treasurer, commissary, attorney-general, should be chosen by joint ballot of both houses. And these and all other elections, especially of representatives and counselors, should be annual, there not being in the whole circle of the sciences a maxim more infallible than this, "where annual elections end, there slavery begins."

These great men, in this respect, should be, once a year,

"Like bubbles on the sea of matter borne, They rise, they break, and to that sea return."

This will teach them the great political virtues of humility, patience, and moderation, without which every man in power becomes a ravenous beast of prey.

This mode of constituting the great offices of state will answer very well for the present; but if by experiment it should be found inconvenient, the legislature may, at its leisure, devise other methods of creating them, by elections of the people at large, as in Connecticut, or it may enlarge the term for which they shall be chosen to seven years, or three years, or for life, or make any other alterations which the society shall find productive of its ease, its safety, its freedom, or, in one word, its happiness.

A rotation of all offices, as well as of representatives and counselors, has many advocates, and is contended for with many plausible arguments. It would be attended, no doubt, with many advantages; and if the society has a sufficient number of suitable characters to supply the great number of vacancies which would be made by such a rotation, I can see no objection to it. These persons may be allowed to serve for three years, and then be excluded three years, or for any longer or shorter term.

Any seven or nine of the legislative council may be made a quorum, for doing business as a privy council, to advise the governor in the exercise of the executive branch of power, and in all acts of state.

The governor should have the command of the militia and of all your armies. The power of pardons should be with the governor and council.

Judges, justices, and all other officers, civil and military, should be nominated and appointed by the governor, with the advice and consent of council, unless you choose to have a government more popular; if you do, all officers, civil and military, may be chosen by joint ballot of both houses; or, in order to preserve the independence and importance of each house, by ballot of one house, concurred in by the other. Sheriffs should be chosen by the freeholders of counties; so should registers of deeds and clerks of counties.

All officers should have commissions, under the hand of the governor and seal of the colony.

The dignity and stability of government in all its branches, the morals of the people, and every blessing of society depend so much upon an upright and skillful administration of justice, that the judicial power ought to be distinct from both the legislative and executive, and independent upon both, that so it may be a check upon both, as both should be checks upon that. The judges, therefore, should be always men of learning and experience in the laws, of exemplary morals, great patience, calmness, coolness, and attention. Their minds should not be distracted with jarring interests; they should not be dependent upon any man, or body of men. To these ends, they should hold estates for life in their offices; or, in other words, their commissions should be during good behavior, and their salaries ascertained and established by law. For misbehavior, the grand inquest of the colony, the house of representatives, should impeach them before the governor and council, where they should have time and opportunity to make their defense; but, if convicted, should be removed from their offices, and subjected to such other punishment as shall be proper.

A militia law, requiring all men, or with very few exceptions besides cases of conscience, to be provided with arms and ammunition, to be trained at certain seasons; and requiring counties, towns, or other small districts, to be provided with public stocks of ammunition and entrenching utensils, and with some settled plans for transporting provisions after the militia, when marched to defend their country against sudden invasions; and requiring certain districts to be provided with field-pieces, companies of matrosses, and perhaps some regiments of light-horse, is always a wise institution, and, in the present circumstances of our country, indispensable.

Laws for liberal education of youth, especially of the lower class of people, are so extremely wise and useful, that, to a humane and generous mind, no expense for this purpose would be thought extravagant.

The very mention of sumptuary laws will excite a smile. Whether our countrymen have wisdom and virtue enough to submit to them, I know not; but the happiness of the people might be greatly promoted by them, and a revenue saved sufficient to carry on this war forever. Frugality is a great revenue, besides curing us of vanities, levities, and fopperies, which are real antidotes to all great, manly, and warlike virtues.

But must not all commissions run in the name of a king? No. Why may they not as well run thus, "The colony of to A.B. greeting," and be tested by the governor?

Why may not writs, instead of running in the name of the king, run thus, "The colony of —to the sheriff," &c., and be tested by the chief justice?

Why may not indictments conclude, "against the peace of the colony of — and the dignity of the same?"

A constitution founded on these principles introduces knowledge among the people, and inspires them with a conscious dignity becoming freemen; a general emulation takes place, which causes good humor, sociability, good manners, and good morals to be general. That elevation of sentiment inspired by such a government, makes the common people brave and enterprising. That ambition which is inspired by it makes them sober, industrious, and frugal. You will find among them some elegance, perhaps, but more solidity; a little pleasure, but a great deal of business; some politeness, but more civility. If you compare such a country with the regions of domination, whether monarchical or aristocratical, you will fancy yourself in Arcadia or Elysium.

If the colonies should assume governments separately, they should be left entirely to their own choice of the forms; and if a continental constitution should be formed, it should be a congress, containing a fair and adequate representation of the colonies, and its authority should sacredly be confined to those cases, namely, war, trade, disputes between colony and colony, the post-office, and the unappropriated lands of the crown, as they used to be called.

These colonies, under such forms of government, and in such a union, would be unconquerable by all the monarchies of Europe.

You and I, my dear friend, have been sent into life at a time when the greatest lawgivers of antiquity would have wished to live. How few of the human race have ever enjoyed an opportunity of making an election of government, more than of air, soil, or climate, for themselves or their children! When, before the present epocha, had three millions of people full power and a fair opportunity to form and establish the wisest and happiest government that human wisdom can contrive? I hope you will avail yourself and your country of that extensive learning and indefatigable industry which you possess, to assist her in the formation of the happiest governments and the best character of a great people. For myself, I must beg you to keep my name out of sight; for this feeble attempt, if it should be known to be mine, would oblige me to apply to myself those lines of the immortal John Milton, in one of his sonnets:—

"I did but prompt the age to quit their clogs By the known rules of ancient liberty, When straight a barbarous noise environs me Of owls and cuckoos, asses, apes, and dogs."

NOTES

PREFACE

1. Scott Liell, *46 Pages: Thomas Paine, Common Sense, and the Turning Point of Independence* (Philadelphia: Running Press, 2003), 18, 131.
2. John Adams, *John Adams: Writings from the New Nation, 1784-1826,* ed. Gordon S. Wood (New York: Library of America, 2016), 438.
3. Thomas Paine, *The Complete Writings of Thomas Paine*, 2 vols., ed. Philip S. Foner (New York: Citadel Press, 1969), 2:916. To this day, this is still a very serviceable collection of Paine's writings, even as new writings of Paine continue to be discovered.
4. Adams, *Writings from the New Nation*, 584.
5. Pauline Maier, *American Scripture: Making the Declaration of Independence* (New York: Alfred A. Knopf, 1997), 91-95.
6. Alpheus Thomas Mason and Gordon E. Baker, *Free Government in the Making* (New York: Oxford University Press, 1985), 86.
7. Ibid., 138.
8. Paine, *Complete Writings*, 2:1491.

CHAPTER ONE: "THE GREAT QUESTION" OF INDEPENDENCE

1. Letter from Abigail Adams to John Adams, 2 March 1776 (electronic edition), Adams Family Papers: An Electronic Archive, Massachusetts Historical Society (hereafter MHS), http://www.masshist.org/digitaladams/archive/doc?id=L17760302aa&bc=%2Fdigitaladams%2Farchive%2Fbrowse%2Fletters_1774_1777.php.
2. John Adams autobiography, pt. 1, "John Adams," through 1776, sheet 23 of 53 (electronic edition), Adams Family Papers: An Electronic Archive, MHS, http://www.masshist.org/digitaladams/archive/doc?id=A1_23&bc=%2Fdigitaladams%2Farchive%2Fbrowse%2Fautobio1.php.
3. Letter from John Adams to Abigail Adams, 19 March 1776 (electronic edition), Adams Family Papers: An Electronic Archive, MHS, http://www.masshist.org/digitaladams/archive/doc?id=L17760319ja&bc=%2Fdigitaladams%2Farchive%2Fbrowse%2Fletters_1774_1777.php.
4. David McCullough, *John Adams* (New York: Simon & Schuster, 2001), 96.
5. Paine, *Complete Writings*, 1:4.
6. Maier, *American Scripture*, 34.
7. Paine, *Complete Writings*, 1:143-144.
8. David McCullough, *1776* (New York: Simon & Schuster, 2005), 11.
9. Liell, *46 Pages*, 14.

10. Library of Congress, "Charles Lee to George Washington, January 24, 1776," *George Washington Papers 1741-1799: Series 4. General Correspondence, 1697-1799.*
11. Founders Online, "From George Washington to Lieutenant Colonel Joseph Reed, January 31, 1776," National Archives, last modified July 12, 2016, http://founders.archives.gov/documents/washington/03-03-02-0163.
12. John Adams, sheet 23, MHS, http://www.masshist.org/digitaladams/archive/doc?id=A1_23&bc=%2Fdigitaladams%2Farchive%2Fbrowse%2Fautobio1.php.
13. Ibid.
14. Ibid.
15. Paine, *Complete Writings,* 2:62.
16. Ibid., 2:78-80.
17. John Adams, sheet 23, MHS, http://www.masshist.org/digitaladams/archive/doc?id=A1_23&bc=%2Fdigitaladams%2Farchive%2Fbrowse%2Fautobio1.php.
18. An examination of the collected works of both authors reveals no evidence for any correspondence between John Adams and Thomas Paine.

CHAPTER TWO: COMMON SENSE

1. Paine, *Complete Writings*, 1:143-144.
2. David Hackett Fischer, *Washington's Crossing* (New York: Oxford University Press, 2004), 139.
3. John Keane, *Tom Paine: A Political Life* (Boston: Little, Brown, 1995), 38.
4. For a discussion of this period in Paine's life, set against eighteenth-century London society and the European Enlightenment, see Craig Nelson, *Thomas Paine: Enlightenment, Revolution, and the Birth of Modern Nations* (New York: Penguin, 2006), 12-50.
5. Paine, *Complete Writings,* 2:9.
6. Ibid., 2:1228
7. Ibid., 2:192.
8. Moncure Daniel Conway, *The Life of Thomas Paine*, 4 vols. (New York: G.P. Putnam's Sons, 1892), 1:67. Conway completed the first thorough biography of Paine and was elected the first president of the Thomas Paine National Historical Association in 1884.
9. For a discussion of Rush's role in encouraging Paine to write *Common Sense*, see David Freeman Hawke, *Paine* (New York: Harper & Row, 1974), 40. Hawke also wrote a biography of Rush. Conway doubts Rush's assertion that he was the source of the title suggestion, though he points out that Paine did say he shared drafts of the tract with "a few" others. Conway, *Life of Thomas Paine*, 1:68. Paine identifies at least one person who saw a draft of portions of *Common Sense* because Paine writes in the second of his *Forester Letters*, published in spring 1776, that he showed "some part" of the pamphlet "while in manuscript" to "a gentleman of known independent principles" who was up for election "for a Burgess of this city [Philadelphia]." The gentleman was David Rittenhouse, a friend of Paine's. Paine, *Complete Writings*, 2:67.

10. Liell, *46 Pages*, 148.
11. Richard Gimbel, *Thomas Paine: A Bibliographical Check List of Common Sense* (New Haven, CT: Yale University Press, 1956).
12. Mason and Baker, *Free Government*, 117.
13. These and the following quotations from *Common Sense* in this chapter are from Paine, *Complete Writings*, 1:3-46.
14. John Adams autobiography, pt. 1, "John Adams," through 1776, sheet 23 of 53 (electronic edition), Adams Family Papers: An Electronic Archive, MHS, http://www.masshist.org/digitaladams/archive/doc?id=A1_23&bc=%2Fdigitaladams%2Farchive%2Fbrowse%2Fautobio1.php.
15. As Harvey Kay noted, this last sentence did not always sit well with opponents of immigration. See Harvey J. Kay, *Thomas Paine and the Promise of America* (New York: Hill and Wang, 2005), 172.
16. Edward S. Corwin, "The Progress of Constitutional Theory between the Declaration of Independence and the Meeting of the Philadelphia Convention," in Gordon S. Wood, ed., *The Confederation and the Constitution: The Critical Issues* (Boston: Brown University Press, 1973), 33.
17. Bernard Bailyn, *The Ideological Origins of the American Revolution* (Cambridge, MA: Harvard University Press, 1967), 17-19.
18. For a discussion of Revolutionary-era nationalists, see Edward J. Larson, *George Washington, Nationalist* (Charlottesville: University Press of Virginia, 2016). Larson continues the tradition of ignoring Paine's role as an early nationalist.
19. Eric Foner, *Tom Paine and Revolutionary America* (New York: Oxford University Press, 1976), 75.
20. Maier, *American Scripture*, 34.

CHAPTER THREE: THOUGHTS ON GOVERNMENT

1. "From John Adams to Horatio Gates, 23 March 1776," Founders Online, National Archives, last modified October 5, 2016, http://founders.archives.gov/documents/Adams/06-04-02-0023.
2. McCullough, *John Adams*, 20.
3. Joseph J. Ellis, *Revolutionary Summer: The Birth of American Independence* (New York: Vintage, 2013), 18.
4. For a background and comparison of the letters and pamphlet, see Adams Family Papers, *Founding Families: Digital Editions of the Papers of the Winthrops and the Adamses*, ed. C. James Taylor (Boston: MHS, 2017), https://www.masshist.org/publications/apde2/view?&id=PJA04dg2. Interestingly, Adams recalled years later, "I wrote my Letter to Mr. Wythe, and it was published in the Beginning of the year 1776 under the Title of 'Thoughts on Government in a Letter from a Gentleman to his Friend.'" See Adams, *Writings from the New Nation*, 479.
5. This and the following quotations from *Thoughts on Government* in this chapter, including a comparison of several paragraphs from Adams's other drafts, are at https://www.masshist.org/publications/apde2/view?&id=PJA04dg2.

6. The phrase "an Empire of Laws, and not of men" is from the English philosopher James Harrington.
7. Ron Chernow, *Alexander Hamilton* (New York: Penguin, 2004), 224.
8. Paine, *Complete Writings*, 2:303.
9. Foner, *Tom Paine*, 117.
10. Ibid, 90.
11. Paine, *Complete Writings*, 1:375.
12. For a discussion of mixed and unmixed government, see Corinne Comstock Weston, *English Constitutional Theory and the House of Lords* (New York: Columbia University Press, 1965), 179.

CHAPTER FOUR: A DECLARATION

1. Paine, *Complete Writings*, 1:39-46. A handy source for the Declaration of Independence, the Articles of Confederation, and the Constitution is R. B. Bernstein, *The Constitution of the United States with the Declaration of Independence and the Articles of Confederation* (New York: Fall River Press, 2012).
2. McCullough, *John Adams*, 107.
3. "V. Preamble to Resolution on Independent Governments, 15 May 1776," Founders Online, National Archives, last modified October 5, 2016, http://founders.archives.gov/documents/Adams/06-04-02-0001-0006.
4. "Resolution Introduced in the Continental Congress by Richard Henry Lee (Virginia) Proposing a Declaration of Independence, June 7, 1776," Avalon Project, Yale Law School, http://avalon.law.yale.edu/18th_century/lee.asp.
5. For Adams's account, see "From John Adams to Timothy Pickering, 6 August 1822," Founders Online, National Archives, last modified October 5, 2016, http://founders.archives.gov/documents/Adams/99-02-02-7674. For Jefferson's account, see Carl Becker, *The Declaration of Independence* (New York: Harcourt, Brace, 1922), ch. 4, 135-193.
6. Maier, *American Scripture*, 126.
7. Jefferson's comment quoted in Nelson, *Thomas Paine*, 93. For an example of writers who have argued that Paine played a direct role in drafting the Declaration of Independence, see Joseph Lewis, *Thomas Paine: Author of the Declaration of Independence* (New York: Free Thought Press Association, 1947).
8. For an argument that the declaration represents more of the thinking of the Scottish Enlightenment than Locke, see Garry Wills, *Inventing America* (New York: Vintage, 1979).
9. For a background discussion of the Declaration of Independence and Jefferson's role in the Committee of Five, see "America's Founding Documents," National Archives, https://www.archives.gov/founding-docs/declaration-history. Also see Becker, *Declaration of Independence*. For a comparison of Jefferson's phrases with Locke's, see John Locke, *Two Treatises of Government*, ed. Peter Laslett (New York: Cambridge University Press, 1990), 414-415n.
10. "From Thomas Jefferson to Henry Lee, 8 May 1825," Founders Online, National Archives, last modified October 5, 2016, http://founders.archives.gov/documents/Jefferson/98-01-02-5212.

11. Bernstein, *Constitution of the United States*, 46-47.
12. For an online version of the *Virginia Declaration of Rights*, see "Virginia Declaration of Rights," America's Founding Documents, National Archives, https://www.archives.gov/founding-docs/virginia-declaration-of-rights.
13. Maier, *American Scripture*, 104.
14. Becker, *Declaration of Independence*, 13.
15. For similarities between Locke's and Jefferson's phrases, see Laslett, *John Locke*, 414-415. Compare the phrases "in the Frame they have been accustom'd to" and "the Forms to which they are accustomed," for example.
16. For years, National Public Radio has read the entire text of the Declaration of Independence over the air on July 4. But in 2017, choosing instead to tweet the entire text in segments of 140 characters each, NPR enraged many in the Twittersphere who thought the declaration's charges against King George were charges NPR was leveling against President Donald Trump.
17. The declaration does not mention the word "states" or, for that matter, even the "United States of America" for the first time; that term can be found as early as 1775 in print. See Maier, *American Scripture*, 44. In fact, the phrase "United States of America, in General Congress, Assembled," is the title given to the government declaring independence in the declaration. That phrase is shortened to "United States in Congress assembled" and repeated several times in the Articles of Confederation. New York abstained from the vote taken on July 2 for independence. It soon agreed with the action taken, however, so the Congress was able to use the word "unanimous" in the declaration by the time it was officially printed.
18. Maier, *American Scripture*, 104.
19. Mason and Baker, *Free Government*, 119.
20. It has been estimated that at the time of the Constitutional Convention in 1787, up to one-third of the white male population of America was disfranchised. See Michael Parenti, *Democracy for the Few* (New York: St. Martin's Press, 1980), 54.
21. Maier, *American Scripture*, 47-96.
22. "From Thomas Jefferson to Samuel Kercheval," July 12, 1816, in Mason and Baker, *Free Government*, 347.

CHAPTER FIVE: THE ALL-BUT-FORGOTTEN CONSTITUTION

1. Montesquieu, *The Spirit of Laws: a Compendium of the First English Edition*, ed. David Wallace Carrithers (Berkeley: University of California Press, 1977), 3.
2. The quotes are in Alpheus Thomas Mason and Richard H. Leach, *In Quest of Freedom* (Englewood Cliffs, NJ: University Press of America, 1973), 18.
3. Bailyn, *Ideological Origins*, 71.
4. See Weston, *English Constitutional Theory*, 179.
5. John Adams diary no. 27, 13 May to 10 September 1776 (electronic edition), Adams Family Papers: An Electronic Archive, MHS, http://www.masshist.org/digitaladams/archive/doc?id=D27&bc=%2Fdigitaladams%2Farchive%2Fbrowse%2Fdiaries_by_date.php, see diary entry on p. 17.

6. Montesquieu, *Spirit of Laws*, 184-185.
7. Benjamin Franklin to Lord Kames, April 11, 1767, in Mason and Baker, *Free Government*, 89.
8. See Gordon Wood, *Revolutionary Characters: What Made the Founders Different* (New York: Penguin, 2006), 146; Ellis, *Revolutionary Summer*, 113.
9. McCullough, *John Adams*, 147.
10. Mason and Baker, *Free Government*, 132.
11. "Articles of Confederation," American Memory, Library of Congress, http://memory.loc.gov/cgi-bin/ampage?collId=llsl&fileName=001/lls l001.db&recNum=127.
12. Corwin, "Process of Constitutional Theory," in Wood, *Confederation and the Constitution*, 28-29.
13. The term "critical period" was coined by Harlan Fiske in the 1880s to describe the near chaos that developed in the national government in the five years after the Articles of Confederation as it tried to confront debtor rebellions, paper money, and states that were "flying off in separate directions." E. James Ferguson, "What Were the Sources of the Constitutional Convention?" in Wood, *Confederation and the Constitution*, 1. It should be noted that not all historians, and Wood is one of these, regard the "critical" years as so critical, that is, in desperate need of a fix. See Gordon S. Wood, "The Articles of Confederation and the Constitution," lecture presented at Humanities Texas Teacher Institute, El Paso, July/August 2010.
14. An abridged version of Adams's *Defence* can be found in Mason and Baker, *Free Government*, 160-169.
15. Joseph Ellis, *Passionate Sage: The Character and Legacy of John Adams* (New York: W. W. Norton, 2001), 148.
16. I have argued elsewhere that one of the often repeated stories, that George Washington ordered words from Paine's *American Crisis Number 1* to be read to his troops prior to crossing the Delaware, is not supported by any direct evidence. See, Jett Conner, "The American Crisis before Crossing the Delaware?," *Journal of the American Revolution* (Feb. 15, 2015), https://allthingsliberty.com /?s=crossing+the+delaware.
17. For a review of the Silas Deane Affair, see Hawke, *Paine*, 81-91.
18. Paine, *Complete Writings*, 2:211-263.
19. Keane, *Tom Paine*, 247-248.
20. For a book on Paine's iron bridges, see Edward G. Gray, *Tom Paine's Iron Bridge: Building a United States* (New York: W. W. Norton, 2016).

CHAPTER SIX: THE FIRST FEDERALIST?

1. Thomas Jefferson to Richard Price, February 1, 1785, Avalon Project, Yale Law School, http://avalon.law.yale.edu/18th_century/let26.asp. Two years earlier, Jefferson had written Edmund Randolph that unless "the band of our confederacy" was strengthened, he feared that the states would go to war with each other "in defiance of Congress." Mason and Baker, *Free Government*, 136.
2. Max Farrand, ed., *The Records of the Federal Convention of 1787*, 3 vols. (New Haven, CT: Yale University Press, 1966), 1:178.

3. Joseph Ellis, *American Creation* (New York: Alfred A. Knopf/Random House, 2007), 103. James Madison deserves the "ultranationalist" label as well, at least on the eve of the Constitutional Convention in 1787, because he wrote that the national government should "have a negative, in all cases whatsoever, on the Legislative acts of the States." Mason and Baker, *Free Government*, 179.
4. "From Alexander Hamilton to James Duane, [3 September 1780]," Founders Online, National Archives, last modified December 6, 2016, http://founders.archives.gov/documents/Hamilton/01-02-02-0838.
5. Jett Conner, "Tom Paine and the Genesis of American Federalism," in Adolph H. Grundman, *The Embattled Constitution: Vital Framework or Convenient Symbol* (Malabar, FL: Robert E. Krieger Publishing, 1986), 17.
6. Chernow, *Alexander Hamilton*, 139.
7. Larson, *George Washington*, 15.
8. Paine, *Complete Writings*, 2:913. The italics are Paine's.
9. Ibid., 1:171.
10. Mason and Baker, *Free Government*, 134.
11. Paine, *Complete Writings*, 2:332-333.
12. Ibid., 2:62. Paine may also have written an anonymous pamphlet that appeared in Philadelphia in June 1776, *Four Letters on Interesting Subjects*, the fourth letter providing an argument for a strong national government. However, the authorship of this pamphlet is still contested. Paine scholar Eric Foner did not believe Paine wrote the pamphlet when he edited a Library of America edition of Paine's collected works and decided not to include it. See Thomas Paine, *Collected Writings,* Library of America No. 76, ed. Eric Foner (New York: Penguin/Putman, 1995). But recently, the Thomas Paine National Historical Association, using new software analyzing writing style and content, determined that the pamphlet was most likely written by Paine. See Thomas Paine, *Four Letters on Interesting Subjects*, Thomas Paine National Historical Association, http://thomaspaine.org/recently-discovered/four-letters-on-interesting-subjects.html.
13. Paine, *Complete Writings*, 1:59-60. Several scholars of Paine have suggested that this is the first time "The United States of America" appeared in print, a claim that perhaps has some merit with respect to Paine's intention to give the new nation a singular name and not use the phrase as it had often appeared before, as a plural description.
14. Ibid., 1:204.
15. Ibid., 1:207.
16. Ibid., 2:347.
17. Ibid., 1:233-234.
18. Ibid., 1:238-239.
19. Ibid., 1:605.
20. Isaac Kramnick, ed., *Thomas Paine: Common Sense* (Baltimore: Penguin, 1976), 46-55.
21. Paine, *Complete Writings*, 2:354-355.
22. Ibid., 2:367.

23. Ibid., 2:374.
24. Edward Mead Earle, *The Federalist: Bicentennial Edition* (Washington, DC: Robert B. Luce, 1976), 53-62.
25. Paine, *Complete Writings*, 2:409.
26. Kay, *Thomas Paine*, 53.
27. Paine, *Complete Writings*, 2:403-404.
28. For an interesting read and thorough analysis of Paine's constitutional thought and what might have happened to American constitutional law if Paine's ideas had prevailed over those of John Marshall, see Robin West, "Tom Paine's Constitution," *Virginia Law Review* 89 (2003): 1413-1461, http://scholarship.law.georgetown.edu/cgi/viewcontent.cgi?article=1285&context=facpub.
29. Foner, *Tom Paine*, 199.
30. Paine, *Complete Writings*, 1:251.
31. M. J. C. Vile, *Constitutionalism and the Separation of Powers*, 2nd ed. (Indianapolis: Liberty Fund, 1998), 138-139, http://oll.libertyfund.org/titles/677.
32. Wood, *Revolutionary Characters*, 179.

EPILOGUE

1. Paine, *Complete Writings,* 2:1498.
2. For an exchange of letters between Paine and Adams on religion, see ibid., 2:1432-1436.
3. Ibid., 2:691.
4. Hawke, *Paine*, 355-356.
5. Ibid., 401.
6. Adams, *Writings from the New Nation*, 306.
7. Paine, *Complete Writings*, 1:xliv.

BIBLIOGRAPHY

As a great help to researchers and readers, many important resources continue to be digitized. Where possible, this book makes use of such resources. Many of the papers of John Adams and family are available, as are those of George Washington and other Revolutionary era figures, in an easily accessed electronic format. Mostly ongoing, much of this work has already taken years. It should be noted that web pages are often updated and therefore links to them sometimes become broken. For a recent collection of the writings of John Adams in book form, see the Library of America series of three volumes on Adams, edited by Gordon S. Wood. Unfortunately, there is no complete, universally recognized and up-to-date collection of Thomas Paine's works in book form. His own personal papers were lost, some during his lifetime and many after his death. And as some of his published materials were written anonymously, attribution is still debated today for some of his writings, though several new works have recently been discovered or attributed to him. The most complete collection of his writings in a single source remains that published by Philip S. Foner in his two-volume set, *The Complete Writings of Thomas Paine*, originally published in 1945. The Thomas Paine National Historical Association has worked to authenticate some of Paine's articles, letters, and tracts, using new style-analysis software. It has digitized his writings as well. But there remains a dispute among scholars about what exactly he wrote, including works previously attributed to him. Perhaps we'll never know for sure.

BOOKS AND ARTICLES

Adams, John. *John Adams: Writings from the New Nation, 1784-1826*. Edited by Gordon S. Wood. New York: Library of America, 2016.

Bailyn, Bernard. *The Ideological Origins of the American Revolution.* Cambridge, MA: Harvard University Press, 1967.

Becker, Carl. *The Declaration of Independence.* New York: Harcourt, Brace, 1922.

Bernstein, R. B. *The Constitution of the United States with the Declaration of Independence and the Articles of Confederation.* New York: Fall River Press, 2012.

Chernow, Ron. *Alexander Hamilton.* New York: Penguin, 2004.

Conner, Jett. "The American Crisis before Crossing the Delaware?," *Journal of the American Revolution* (Feb. 25, 2015), allthingsliberty.com.

———. "Tom Paine and the Genesis of American Federalism." In Adolph H. Grundman, *The Embattled Constitution: Vital Framework or Convenient Symbol.* Malabar, FL: Robert E. Krieger, 1986.

Conway, Moncure Daniel. *The Life of Thomas Paine.* 4 vols. New York: G.P. Putnam's Sons, 1892.

Corwin, Edward S. "The Progress of Constitutional Theory between the Declaration of Independence and the Meeting of the Philadelphia Convention." In Gordon S. Wood, ed., *The Confederation and the Constitution: The Critical Issues.* Boston: Brown University Press, 1973.

Earle, Edward Mead. *The Federalist: Bicentennial Edition.* Washington, DC: Robert B. Luce, 1976.

Ellis, Joseph J. *American Creation.* New York: Alfred A. Knopf/Random House, 2007.

———. *Passionate Sage: The Character and Legacy of John Adams.* New York: W. W. Norton, 2001.

———. *Revolutionary Summer: The Birth of American Independence.* New York: Vintage, 2013.

Farrand, Max, ed. *The Records of the Federal Convention of 1787.* 3 vols. New Haven, CT: Yale University Press, 1966.

Ferguson, E. James. "What Were the Sources of the Constitutional Convention?" In Gordon Wood, ed., *The Confederation and the Constitution: The Critical Issues.* Providence: Brown University Press, 1973.

Fischer, David Hackett. *Washington's Crossing.* New York: Oxford University Press, 2004.

Foner, Eric. *Tom Paine and Revolutionary America*. New York: Oxford University Press, 1976.

Gimbel, Richard. *Thomas Paine: A Bibliographical Check List of Common Sense*. New Haven, CT: Yale University Press, 1956.

Gray, Edward G. *Tom Paine's Iron Bridge: Building a United States*. New York: W. W. Norton, 2016.

Hawke, David Freeman. *Paine*. New York: Harper & Row, 1974.

Kay, Harvey. *Thomas Paine and the Promise of America*. New York: Hill and Wang, 2005.

Keane, John. *Tom Paine, a Political Life*. New York: Little, Brown, 1995.

Kramnick, Isaac. *Thomas Paine: Common Sense*. Baltimore: Penguin, 1976.

Larson, Edward J. *George Washington, Nationalist*. Charlottesville: University Press of Virginia, 2016.

Lewis, Joseph. *Thomas Paine: Author of the Declaration of Independence*. New York: Free Thought Press Association, 1947.

Liell, Scott. *46 Pages: Thomas Paine, Common Sense, and the Turning Point of Independence*. Philadelphia: Running Press, 2003.

Locke, John. *Two Treatises of Government*. Edited by Peter Laslett. New York: Cambridge University Press, 1990.

Maier, Pauline. *American Scripture: Making the Declaration of Independence*. New York: Alfred A. Knopf, 1997.

Mason, Alpheus Thomas, and Gordon E. Baker. *Free Government in the Making*. 4th ed. New York: Oxford University Press, 1985.

Mason, Alpheus Thomas, and Richard H. Leach. *In Quest of Freedom*. Englewood Cliffs, NJ: University Press of America, 1973.

McCullough, David. *John Adams*. New York: Simon & Schuster, 2001.

———. *1776*. New York: Simon & Schuster, 2005.

Montesquieu. *The Spirit of Laws: a Compendium of the First English Edition*. Edited by David Wallace Carrithers. Berkeley: University of California Press, 1977.

Nelson, Craig. *Thomas Paine: Enlightenment, Revolution, and the Birth of Modern Nations*. New York: Penguin, 2006.

Paine, Thomas. *Collected Writings*. Edited by Eric Foner. Library of America, No. 76. New York: Penguin/Putman, 1995.

———. *The Complete Writings of Thomas Paine*. 2 vols. Edited by Philip S. Foner. New York: Citadel Press, 1969.

———. *Four Letters on Interesting Subjects*. Thomas Paine National Historical Association, www.thomaspaine.org.

Parenti, Michael. *Democracy for the Few*. New York: St. Martin's Press, 1980.

Vile, M. J. C. *Constitutionalism and the Separation of Powers*. 2nd ed. Reprint, Indianapolis: Liberty Fund, 1998. http://oll.libertyfund.org/titles/677.

West, Robin. "Tom Paine's Constitution." *Virginia Law Review* 89 (2003): 1413-1461.

Weston, Corinne Comstock. *English Constitutional Theory and the House of Lords*. New York: Columbia University Press, 1965.

Wills, Garry. *Inventing America*. New York: Vintage, 1979.

Wood, Gordon S. "The Articles of Confederation and the Constitution." Lecture presented at Humanities Texas Teacher Institute, El Paso, July/August, 2010.

———, ed. *The Confederation and the Constitution: The Critical Issues*. Boston: Brown University Press, 1973.

———. *Revolutionary Characters: What Made the Founders Different*. New York: Penguin, 2006.

ELECTRONIC RESOURCES

Adams Family Papers: An Electronic Archive. Massachusetts Historical Society. http://www.masshist.org/digitaladams/.

———. *Founding Families: Digital Editions of the Papers of the Winthrops and the Adamses*. Edited by C. James Taylor. Boston: Massachusetts Historical Society, 2017. www.masshist.org/apde2/.

The Avalon Project. Yale Law School. http://avalon.law.yale.edu/.

Founders Online. National Archives. http://founders.archives.gov/.

George Washington Papers 1741-1799. Library of Congress. https://www.loc.gov/collections/george-washington-papers.

Journal of the American Revolution. https://allthingsliberty.com/.

Liberty Fund Books. www.libertyfund.org/books.aspx.

Thomas Paine National Historical Association. www.thomaspaine.org.

INDEX